**NEA
EARLY CHILDHOOD
EDUCATION SERIES**

D1028399

Play's Place in
Public Education
for Young Children

Victoria Jean Dimidjian
Editor

A NATIONAL EDUCATION ASSOCIATION
P U B L I C A T I O N

Printing History
   First Printing: February 1992
   Second Printing: August 1993

Note
The opinions expressed in this publication should not be construed as representing the policy or position of the National Education Association. Materials published by the NEA Professional Library are intended to be discussion documents for teachers who are concerned with specialized interests of the profession.

Library of Congress Cataloging-in-Publication Data

Play's place in public education for young children / Victoria Jean
    Dimidjian, editor
        p.   cm.—(NEA early childhood education series)
    Includes bibliographical references
    ISBN 0–8106–0364–0
    1. Play—United States. 2. Early childhood education—United
States.   I. Dimidjian, Victoria Jean. II. Series. Early childhood
education series (Washington, D.C.)
    LB1137.P558   1992
    372.21—dc20   91–27420
                                         20   CIP

CONTENTS

Part II. Curriculum and the Place of Play in Educating Young Children

PREFACE

To encounter a "true teacher" is a transforming experience. Any student who has been lucky enough to work under the thoughtful and stimulating guidance of a wise educator never forgets the impact of such a privilege. This book is dedicated to the memory of Margaret B. McFarland, Professor Emerita of the University of Pittsburgh, a teacher who touched my mind and my life with her quietly stated, incisive wisdom.

I met her at eight o'clock one Friday morning. I came into her office for a graduate school interview and left with the conviction that I had found someone who could teach me about children and who also understood and could teach me more about myself. As I worked with Margaret—first as a student, then as a staff member at the university, then as a colleague (but one who never found it comfortable to call her anything other than "Dr. McFarland" to her peering eyes)—I never stopped learning from her queries and her gentle insistence on exploring each complex facet of children's growth. She was the most giving, understanding, responsive, and yet intensely private teacher/ mentor I could imagine. Her passing in 1988 still leaves an emptiness, although her memory—and sometimes even the phrases and stories she used in her teaching—still comes to mind often.

But her legacy lives on. This book contains many contributions by individuals who were her colleagues, students, or both, reflecting her understanding and compassion for children that were a part of the Pittsburgh professional community for decades. She—who could speak so empathically to a three-year-old at the sand table or to a seminar of 30-year-old psychiatric residents reviewing records of children's play—never seemed to miss an opportunity to deepen the life process by truly engaging with all her intellect and heart simultaneously. And just at the moment of insight, just when you saw a new possibility or grasped a new idea, the quick drift of her smile and playful flicker of her eyes told you she knew just the leap that you had made and, oh, she liked that new step so very much. So this book is dedicated to her and to those like her, the few-times-in-a-lifetime "true teachers" that we all need so very much.

—Victoria Jean Dimidjian

Part I

Connecting Theory on Play's Place in Early Education to Today's Classrooms for Young Children

Part I
INTRODUCTION

by Victoria Jean Dimidjian

As far back as human history is recorded we find evidence that children played, valued playthings, and created special words and products and rituals while engaged in "play."

Yet for most of human history the opportunity to spend extended periods "at play" was severely limited, possible only for the children of the most privileged classes of society. Historians studying childhood (Aries 1962; Sommerville 1982) have highlighted the recent emergence of the belief that all children should have the opportunity for play before being pushed into the world of work, of economic productivity, and of societal responsibility. Perhaps part of today's distrust about the importance of play in the learning process is rooted in the centuries when play was denied to most, a benefit to only the very affluent and educated.

Whatever the reasons, both adults and children can easily identify and describe when they are "at play"; thus the need to define this term may at first seem unnecessary. Yet some teachers today say that "play is the work of the child" while others contrast the definition of play with that of work, ensuring the dichotomy between "important" work and "only-when-the-work-is-done" play—and therefore the possible danger of leaving play at the early childhood classroom door. What exactly does this word PLAY really mean?

Conversing with children can help to clarify the issue.

Recently I asked four children—ages 4, 7, 8, and 10—to talk with me about "work and play and going to school." The holiday season had thrown relatives and neighbors together. Thus nearly 11-year-old Katie listened while the others talked, starting with her younger brother. Four-year-old Jack attends a child care center where, he says, he plays every day. Then he enthusiastically describes his favorite games of dressing up in superhero garb, working with the blocks and cars that he wishes he had at home, and working on the computers (which he does have at home). His 8-year-old cousin Nicholas interrupts, telling him that all those don't count " 'cause you don't go to real school." But when I ask Nick, he does recall his kindergarten "being lots of fun 'cause we did stuff like that." What is school like now? "Oh, pretty boring, we just sit and work all day long. Hate it now, after New Year's when we have to start it again." Seven-year-old neighbor Alejandro nods, and when I ask him what he likes to do best at school, he quickly replies, "Oh, gym, for sure, and if we get time on the computers, and sometimes she has us writing our own stories and stuff like that." Now Katie joins the conversation. "Yeah, Nick, you're lucky you've got Mrs. Ramos this year. She's pretty fun. I hope I get Mrs. Smith next year; everybody says she has lots of different stuff to do in her room, not just boring work all the time."

"Katie, would you call that stuff play?" I ask.

"Well, I don't know, not really 'cause play is what we do after school, isn't it? But it's kind of like play, I guess. Like where she has game shows where you have to beat the teacher at stuff like naming the capitals of the countries faster than she does. Or making your own scrapbook of drawings and newspaper stories about a country. Or a group of kids will make one continent in salt and flour, and then they'll write a news report about what happened there every day for about a month and pretend to be on TV sometimes for the rest of the class. They got to videotape a show every day—that's neat, huh?" Katie becomes animated telling us about all the things she's heard the sixth graders talk about.

Katie's words express the mental division, the nearly adultlike thinking, that she has made between the domains of her world where work/tedium/school/public life activities and those of play/interest/enthusiasm/home/private life activities are clearly separated. Most adults would agree with her, that life's experiences have confirmed that activities in the "public" arenas of classroom or workplaces have tended to be routine, often boring, rarely exciting our earnest interest. By adulthood we have come to accept that much of our daily life is repetitive, a routine to be done adequately, even diligently, but without much individual creativity and ingenuity.

Yet Katie also has had experiences when the walls between the two domains come down, when learning in the classroom becomes intensely involving and pleasurable. She hopes for that opportunity next year, and she tells her three younger listeners about it, orienting them to what she now sees as "special" learning that she seems to have concluded can "sometimes" happen at school. So, too, adults look for the opportunities for workplace challenges demanding thought, creativity, and individual initiative. The American business world today is refashioning its structure and retooling its work force so that more opportunities for optimal engagement can occur. So, too, must education move from the assembly-line mentality toward the individually challenged yet collectively accountable mode of instruction if children are to be adequately prepared for functioning in the social and work worlds of the twenty-first century.

Education to challenge the whole student—linguistically, socially, physically, analytically, creatively, emotionally—and then to *validate outcomes of learning processes* that meet that challenge—has never been needed more than today. Whether in a kindergarten or a college classroom, truly meaningful education actively engages the physical, mental, verbal, and social/emotional domains; it poses integrated, activity-based challenges for those domains to master, apply, and ultimately creatively reintegrate content. For the professional teacher or the college student, the challenges are primarily met under the guidance of the synthesizing intellect while necessarily engaging the whole personality. But for the young child whose acquisition of understanding is still so rooted in the body and the web of emotional bonds one has with others, knowledge is best gained through a process of moving, speaking, doing with others, discovering for oneself, and mastering new challenges in an environment where play and work are one domain. *And* where the teacher engages with children so that the joys of playing and the accomplishments of working are simultaneously achieved.

TABLE 1

Play	Work
Internally motivated	Externally motivated
Self-initiated and self-ended	Starts/stops according to workplace schedule
Open-ended process	Goal-oriented product
Internally controlled	Externally controlled
Contains elements of make-believe, fantasy, "as-if" thinking/creation	Reality-based, "as-is" thinking
Expresses positive emotion: pleasure, joy, and controlled excitement	Channels feeling into productive end results
Internally valued and evaluated	Externally evaluated and rewarded by others
Contributes to establishing internal locus of control	Strengthens external locus of control

(Adapted from Neumann 1971; Garvey 1977; and Fein 1981.)

For early childhood teachers to do so means they must have transcended the gaps that currently exist among traditional adult barriers known as "play" and "work" and "learning." Traditionally during much of this century, play has been defined as the activity children do *until* they are "ready to begin real work" or *after* they have successfully completed schoolwork tasks, and school curriculum has pushed play farther and farther from the classroom door. Playground play, yes; classroom play, no. This division seems at first supported by researchers on play who tend to contrast the domains of "work" with those of "play" in defining the meaning of this problematic four-letter word. Surely Table 1 at first seems to validate such division. However, this table is designed to convey the mentality of mature humans who have the capacity to both DO and EVALUATE THE DOING simultaneously, who have reached what Piaget has described as the stage of formal operations, and who can readily categorize their activities into boxes of "working hard now" or "at play, on vacation, etc." as they are engaged in them.

14

This simultaneous capacity for thinking-doing is not developed in young children like four-year-old Jack or even completely developed in seven-year-old Nicky. The child of this age—the preoperational child—engages in walking to the store, drawing a picture, scrubbing the bathroom wall with mom, helping dad rake up grass, and trying to join in the Nintendo play with the same enthusiasm, with the same playful impulse. What is "work" versus "play" becomes distinguishable only slowly during the years from three to eight, as any parent or teacher with extensive experience with this age group can validate. This is why, for example, the chore of "clean up" can be an enjoyable game if adults set up the process skillfully, or why a long monotonous car ride can be transformed by word game or singing or "what can you see?" into a fun game with young children. Slowly the domains of "real" from "fantasy" and "play" from "work" become built as the child readies for the move from the preoperational to the concrete operational stage, to use Piaget's framework. Moving the young child prematurely from the world of play, drawing an adult boundary that fits the young child into the world of work, may prevent important cognitive, emotional, and social growth from coalescing.

The most comprehensive, moving analysis of play's importance in the life cycle of human growth and development is Dorothy and Jerome Singer's *The House of Make-Believe* (1990). In examining the dynamic connection between cognitive and affective growth in the early years that is best nurtured by environments with people and props ready to put to use in play, these authors state:

> *Whatever the limits of the research literature and the clear need for much more investigation, we cannot avoid the belief that imaginative play serves important purposes in the emergence of the psychologically complex and adaptable person. Individual differences in the frequency and variety of such play seem to be associated not only with richer and more complex language but also with a greater potential for cognitive differentiation, divergent thought, impulse control, self-entertainment,*

emotional expressiveness, and, perhaps, self-aware-ness. The training studies on the whole suggest that there are wonderful opportunities . . . to foster thematic play and thus to assist children in fuller cognitive growth and emotional adaptability. Imaginative play is fun, but in the midst of the joys of making believe, children may also be preparing for the reality of more effective lives. (Singer and Singer 1990, 151–52)

The Singers and other researchers examining adult development (Levinson 1980; Smelser and Erikson 1980) have emphasized the need for the maintenance of "play" during later childhood, adolescence, and mature years, even revising Freud's "criteria for healthy adulthood" to expand from simply the capacities to love and to work to also include the capacity to play, to re-create the self throughout the long cycle of generativity.

Bridging the two domains of work and play—which must be a conscious effort in adulthood—occurs naturally in the early years, so much so that some writers have called play "the natural work of the child." To my mind, however, that statement has been misunderstood and misapplied in the last decade in many educational settings. Play is not simply an easy way to "get children to like academic work and do more of it at an earlier age." That view sees the function of the classroom as providing play only until the child is ready to "really learn," a view that David Elkind (1981) and Neil Postman (1984) correctly warned produces hurried, pressured, dependent followers rather than self-confident thinkers. Elkind (1987) further examined the "miseducation" of young children being carried out with all good intentions but without thorough understanding of child development as the theoretical basis for curriculum; and many others (e.g., Suransky 1982; Winn 1983) have affirmed his concerns. Elkind's latest work, *Perspectives on Early Childhood Education* (1991), addresses the challenges facing the early educator today who is attempting to provide the most developmentally appropriate environment possible for young children to play/learn/work in an integrated fashion.

In Part I of this volume the contributors address a similar theme: the need for thorough integration of child development research with daily classroom practice so that every hour of every day will provide play and learning opportunities through developmentally appropriate activities. In the opening chapter, "Play in School? Yes, We're Serious," Pellegrini and Dressden emphasize the importance of this integration. These researchers in early childhood/reading explore the absolute necessity of play-based learning. Fein's research on play has been seminal for the past three decades; her chapter on play and development succinctly summarizes the importance of play in the interrelated domains of the growing, thinking, speaking, and feeling child. Then Curry, Sapp, and Arnaud each examine separate age groups within the four- to eight-year division, known in most school districts today as "Early Childhood." Each author illustrates the integration of child development research and application to work with young children in classrooms and child care environments. Following Arnaud's work, West illustrates the importance of play in one Tampa school's second grade setting. Finally, Rogers and Sharapan, Pittsburgh neighbors of young children, reflect on children's play and development.

Chapter 1

PLAY IN SCHOOL?
YES, WE'RE SERIOUS

by Anthony D. Pellegrini
and Jana Dressden

The idea that play has a role in school settings is probably questionable to a large segment of our population, both professional educators and lay persons alike. It is probably questionable to the extent that Americans generally seem to think that *more* basic instruction is needed for us, as a nation, to compete in the international marketplace. The current metaphor for the education of children in the United States continues to be an assembly line in which children are viewed as incomplete products (or unfinished adults), with knowledge being conveyed by teachers in the most efficient manner as quickly as possible so that children can duplicate the "adult model" as soon as possible. Efficiency is typically defined as more time spent in direct instruction, longer school days, and students' executing tasks in prespecified ways.

Play is, seemingly, the direct opposite of this scenario. In play, children, not adults, define the nature of the task at hand and how to complete it—if, indeed, it is to be completed. After all, how often do children "complete" the block structures they repeatedly build up and knock down? Further, play is inefficient and "uneconomical" to the extent that time and movement are exaggerated with little apparent approximation of a finished product. This characterization of play leads to the belief that it would actually interfere with education, and consequently should be kept out of schools.

In this chapter we will argue that play does have a real place in school. First, we will define fantasy play, an important type of play in primary school (kindergarten through grade two). By describing the fantasy of primary school children we can begin to design developmentally appropriate curriculum for them. Because of space limitations, we will not describe the types of play exhibited by older children. A thorough review of that literature can be found in Pellegrini and Boyd (in press).

In the second section of this chapter we will show the ways in which fantasy play is related to school performance. Results are presented from the large body of empirical research into the effects of play on aspects of children's social and cognitive status.

WHAT IS PLAY?

This seems like a simple enough question, answerable by both lay person and professional alike (Smith and Vollstedt 1985). Indeed, at the most general level people can discriminate play from nonplay. Problems arise, however, when these same observers are asked to say *specifically* what about the behaviors they observe is playful or nonplayful. The point is that specific definitions are important because, as we will see later, only specific aspects of play are correlated with educational outcomes. For example, disagreement and its resolution between players are two important aspects of social fantasy play that relate to children's story comprehension; verbally encoding the story is less important. Therefore, conflict and resolution seem to be important for aspects of story comprehension; consequently, play's use should be expanded in the curriculum.

In this chapter we will describe the form of *fantasy play* that is most common during the early elementary school years. Fantasy play will be defined according to structural dimensions and multiple criteria. (See Martin and Caro 1985; Pellegrini and Boyd in press, for extended discussions of definitional issues.)

Fantasy play is probably the clearest example of play and the form most thoroughly researched (see Pellegrini and Boyd in press; Rubin, Fein, and Vandenberg 1983). Children begin to engage in fantasy play during the second year of life; fantasy increases in frequency of occurrence for the next three to four years and then declines (Fein 1981). Further, of all forms of play observed, fantasy accounts for 10 to 17 percent of preschoolers' play and about 33 percent of kindergartners' play. Few data exist beyond the kindergarten period. The reason for this is probably because play, especially fantasy, is viewed as antithetical to schooling; therefore, little opportunity exists to observe it.

Generally, fantasy involves make-believe; it has been defined *structurally,* following Piaget (1962) and Fein (1981), as including objects and sequential combinations. *Decontextualized behaviors* involve taking a familiar behavior or set of behaviors, such as those related to eating, out of that context—for example, using those eating behaviors without food in a housekeeping corner. *Self-other relations* indicate that children's fantasy is first aimed at self as the actor—for example, a child pretending to be a mother—and then having others take on fantasy roles—having a doll serve as a pretend mother.

Substitute objects relate to the level of abstraction of children's fantasy transformations. More specifically, children's initial transformations are dependent upon objects; for example, a child may need an empty cup to give her doll a drink. Later, these transformations are not dependent upon objects; for example, children typically use language to represent a physically absent prop ("This is her cup" or "I'll give her a drink now") and an empty hand to give a drink. Further, children also use language to define roles ("I'll be the mother and you be the daddy") and situations ("Let's play hospital").

Sequential combinations involve the weaving of these individual transformations into integrated play themes; for example, a child may feed her baby, *then* change its diaper, *then* change its clothes, *and then* go shopping.

Generally, by the time children enter school, they are capable of high levels of fantasy; that is, their fantasy contains all the structural dimensions outlined. Indeed, research has shown that this process is well in place by the time children are three years old (Pellegrini 1987).

Fantasy can also be defined according to *multiple criteria.* (See Krasnor and Pepler 1980 and Smith and Vollstedt 1985 for discussions of multiple criteria definitions.) This approach recommends that behaviors be rated as more or less fantastic according to the number of criteria met; for example, a behavior that meets three criteria is considered more playful than one that meets two criteria. Accordingly behaviors should not be rated either as play or not play. The criteria include the following:

1. *Nonlaterality* simply involves make-believe, where one thing represents something else.
2. *Intrinsic motivation* suggests that children play because they want to do so, not because others tell them to.
3. *Attention to means* further suggests that the process of play, not some end product, is important.
4. *What can it do?* has children exploring the attributes of objects; *What can I do with it?* has children subordinating those object attributes to play themes.
5. *Freedom from external rules* means that children's play does not follow externally predefined rules; it follows rules that they establish. For example, when children play school, their role enactments generally follow specific rules as they have understood them, such as "Teachers give directions and children follow them."
6. *Active engagement* means that children themselves determine the nature of their play.

Research indicates that fantasy episodes that contain more of these criteria are considered more playful than episodes with fewer criteria (Smith and Vollstedt 1985). Further, the nonlaterality criterion is considered the most important in discriminating play bouts.

EFFECTS OF FANTASY
ON CHILDREN'S SOCIAL COGNITIVE STATUS

Inferences about *the effects* of play can be made from two types of research. Longitudinal research measures play at point 1 and social cognitive status at point 2; experimental manipulation studies expose children to treatments containing different aspects of play and measure the relative effect of each treatment on social cognition. Discussion of an illustrative longitudinal study and an experimental study follows.

In a study examining the relations between the level of object substitutions (see above definition) exhibited at age three and a half and writing status (the ability to write words in conventional orthography) at age five, researchers (Galda, Pellegrini, and Cox 1989; Pellegrini and Galda in press) found that level of substitutions in fantasy predicted early writing status. The idea here is that both fantasy and writing use symbolic media (i.e., fantasy transformations and words, respectively) to represent and convey ideas. Preschoolers seem to learn and practice this in fantasy play. Facility for using symbols, then, may be developed through fantasy play and applied to early writing.

In two experimental studies involving kindergartners through second graders, we examined the extent to which aspects of thematic fantasy play, or play about fictional characters like the Three Bears, affected comprehension of the stories enacted (Pellegrini 1984a). The first interesting finding was that children in adult-led versus peer-led play groups enacted and recalled the stories equally well. In short, by the time children are in kindergarten they are very capable of enacting fantasy themes. Indeed, we have observational data suggesting that adults actually *inhibit* children's enactment of fantasy play (Pellegrini 1984b).

The second interesting finding was that thematic fantasy training is more effective with kindergarten children than with first and second graders. Again, this finding points to fantasy being developmentally appropriate for younger (five-year-old) children.

Older children (grades 7 through 12) seem to learn as effectively when each child discusses the book from his or her point of view and how that view is different from and similar to the views of others in the group. In short, having children reconstruct stories from different perspectives helps them understand them. Younger children (ages three to six) go through this same process—enacting, disagreeing, and reaching compromise over role interpretation—when they engage in fantasy.

23

To conclude, we have shown how fantasy relates to aspects of children's cognitive status in school. Other aspects of play, such as rough-and-tumble play, are more common in the middle and later elementary school years and also relate to children's social competence. (See Pellegrini 1989 for a discussion of the role of rough-and-tumble play in elementary school.) Further, we know that children seem to "need" recess and that their behavior at recess is related to aspects of school achievement (Pellegrini 1989). Space limitations prevent a discussion of these other aspects of play. But, based on decades of solid research, we can state that play is educationally beneficial to children; consequently, it deserves a more prominent role in the elementary school curriculum.

REFERENCES

Clay, M. 1972. *Concepts of Print.* Auckland, N.Z.: Heinemann.

Fein, G. 1981. Pretend Play: An Integrative Review. *Child Development* 52: 1095–1118.

Galda, L.; Pellegrini, A. D.; and Cox, S. 1989. A Short-Term Longitudinal Study of Preschoolers' Emergent Literacy. *Research in the Teaching of English* 23: 292–309.

Krasnor, L., and Pepler, D. 1980. The Study of Children's Play. In *Children's Play,* edited by K. Rubin, 85–95. San Francisco: Jossey-Bass.

Martin, P., and Caro, T. 1985. On the Functions of Play and Its Role in Behavioral Development. In *Advances in the Study of Behavior,* vol. 15, edited by J. Rosenblatt, C. Beer, M. C. Busnel, and P. Slater, 59–103. New York: Academic Press.

Pellegrini, A. 1984a. Identifying Causal Elements in the Thematic Fantasy Play Paradiagram. *American Educational Research Journal* 21: 691–703.

———. 1984b. The Social Cognitive Ecology of Preschool Classrooms. *International Journal of Behavioral Development* 7: 321–32.

———. 1987. The Effects of Play Concepts on the Development of Children's Verbalized Fantasy. *Semiotica* 65: 285–93.

Pellegrini, A. D. 1989. Children's Rough-and-Tumble Play: Issues in

Categorization and Functions. *Educational Policy* 3: 389–400.

Pellegrini, A. D., and Boyd, B. In press. The Educational and Developmental Roles of Play in Early Education. In *Handbook of Research in Early Childhood Education,* edited by B. Spodek. New York: Macmillan.

Pellegrini, A. D., and Galda, L. In press. Longitudinal Relations Among Preschool Children's Symbolic Play, Linguistic Verbs, and Emergent Literacy. In *Play and Early Literacy,* edited by J. Christie. Albany: State University of New York Press.

Piaget, J. 1962. *Play, Dreams and Imitation in Childhood.* New York: Norton.

Rubin, K.; Fein, G.; and Vandenberg, B. 1983. Play. In *Handbook of Child Psychology. Vol. 4. Socialization, Personality and Social Development,* edited by P. H. Mussen and E. M. Hetherington, 693–774. New York: Wiley.

Smith, P. K., and Vollstedt, R. 1985. On Defining Play: An Empirical Study of the Relationship Between Play and Various Play Criteria. *Child Development* 56: 1042–50.

Chapter 2

PLAY AND DEVELOPMENT

by Greta G. Fein

"Play" is a small word, only four letters long. Children may be playing when they manipulate objects, climb walls, or tumble in the autumn leaves. Yet philosophers debate its meaning, researchers study its forms and functions, and teachers ponder its place in the curriculum. In play, children solve self-imposed problems. Some of these problems are simple and others are awesomely complex. Some are social and some are material; some are imitative and some are original. Even though researchers distinguish particular forms—functional play, rough-and-tumble play, constructive play, pretend play, and games (Pellegrini 1988; Rubin, Fein, and Vandenberg 1983)—one form often blends into another. Two children wrestling in the leaves (rough-and-tumble play) become a cowboy and a monster (pretend play); one then joins some friends at the slide and the other runs to a swing (functional play). These varied forms have different functions—social engagement, symbolic expression, motor activity. Each form contributes to children's development.

One of these forms, pretend play, has been studied in great depth. Provocative ideas culled from Piaget (1962), Vygotsky (1967), Bateson (1955), and Mead (1934) have helped to produce conceptual and procedural tools for investigating developmental sequences, individual differences, and the contributions of adults, peers, and materials to the elaboration of this behavior. The effort has yielded a stable body of facts and useful conjectures about the cognitive, social, and linguistic competence of young children who engage in pretending (Bretherton 1984; Fein 1981; Rubin, Fein, and Vandenberg 1983).

As Vygotsky (1967) suggested, pretend play may well be a spontaneous childhood activity in which children function at their highest level of competence. Vygotsky makes a distinction

27

between what a child can accomplish under the best, most supportive circumstances and what the same child can accomplish when these supportive circumstances are not present. The spread between unsupported and supported performance is called the "zone of proximal development," or ZPD. Sometimes a child's best performance occurs when the child is interacting with a supportive adult who knows how to "scaffold" the child's problem-solving efforts. The adult withdraws assistance as the child learns how to solve the problem alone. Best performance thus becomes part of the child's regular repertoire.

A child's best performance may also occur during play with peers. In pretend play, this best performance is likely to reflect a child's highest level of symbolic and social competence. Play thus gives the teacher an opportunity to assess a child's competence under optimizing conditions. It also gives the child an opportunity to function at her or his highest symbolic and social level. Using emerging competencies in play is a first step toward consolidating them for use in less supportive activities.

Let me use a brief example to illustrate some dimensions of the symbolic and social competence associated with pretend play. The following pretend sequence took place in a classroom of four-year-olds. As the play began four children were in a wooden rocking boat: Kevin, Camille, Yale, and Stephanie. Here are the first three cycles of a ten-cycle sequence.

Cycle I

Camille to Kevin: Last time we were in this rocket boat there was a worm.

Kevin *(Alarmed)*: There's two bloodsuckers and a spider on the boat!

Camille *(Alarmed):* Yeah, and it's a big spider. You can't jump out. I'm going to jump out and get a sword! *(Both children get out of the boat and chop at it with invisible swords. They return to the boat after 15 seconds.)*

Cycle II

Camille: There's a spider! *(Points at bottom of boat)*

Kevin: There's two bloodsuckers. *(Looks at bottom of boat)*

Camille: Put your feet up quick!

Kevin: *(Ignores her)*

Cycle III

Yale: I'm He-Man! *(Stands up)*

Kevin: I'm Skeletor with his terrible sword! *(Also stands up)*

Camille: *(Jumps out of the boat; puts her foot on the rim)*

Kevin: Get! Get! Get bloodsucker! *(Brushes at Camille's shoe with his hand)*

In later cycles, the children transform the creatures into crocodiles, sharks, and back again into bloodsuckers and a big spider. In the last cycle, toothpicks from the art shelf become "blisters," which the children use as darts to attack the sharks. What does research tell us about the developmental competencies displayed in this sequence?

SYMBOLIC COMPETENCE

Pretend play develops in an ordered sequence, beginning roughly at about 12 months of age (Belsky and Most 1981; Nicolich 1977). Several processes make up this development. One process is *decontextualization.* In the second of year of life, children discover that it is possible to sleep without actually sleeping, or eat without eating. A person's behavior can be detached from physical states of tiredness or hunger. Children then discover that a word or a gesture of sleeping stands for this event. Words and gestures are now used to represent real or imagined feelings and events.

When children pretend that bloodsuckers and spiders are in a toy boat and that crocodiles and sharks are in the water, they are representing these things along with the emotions that these things elicit (Fein 1975; 1989). The children have *transformed* the immediate environment to suit the purposes of their play. Sometimes these transformations are *material,* such as when the children use real toothpicks as dartlike weapons to attack the sharks. In cycles I to III, the transformations are *ideational* (Matthews 1977). The creatures and the swords are completely imaginary. The children recognize at that moment that the creatures are mental entities rather than actual entities in the immediate environment.

In the bloodsucker sequence, material and ideational transformations are supported by the peer group. The most mature players (Camille and Kevin) keep the game moving with recurring moments of excitement. One transformation leads to another, encouraging each child to think about the most dreadful, small and large creatures imaginable. Together and cooperatively, perhaps at the upper boundaries of the ZPD, the children weave these represented creatures, weapons, and actions into a collective narrative. This aspect of pretend calls upon processes that are central in classroom speech, emergent literacy, and, eventually, reading (Pellegrini 1986).

INTRAPERSONAL COMPETENCE

Decentration refers to the child's understanding of self in relation to others. Decentration begins to emerge in the latter part of the second year. It is a fundamental social process: the child establishes a personal identity and, at the same time, recognizes that others have different identities, and thus different points of view that can be compared and related to one's own

(Fein and Schwartz 1986; Rubin and Howe 1986). In pretend, children assume or enact roles that place strong demands upon the child's concepts of self and of others. Kevin is able to declare himself "Skeletor" and still know that he is Kevin. The children behave toward their symbolized adversaries in role-appropriate ways. Kevin brushes the bloodsucker from Camille's shoe; "Skeletor" uses a sword to combat the crocodile.

In some pretend sequences *role enactments* call for an even greater stretch to the upper limits of the ZPD. In these enactments, role relationships *between the children* are reciprocal: a pretend mother feeds a pretend baby. Roles are not only reciprocal, but they intersect: the pretend mother interacts with the pretend father as a wife, with the baby-sitter as an employer, and with the baby as a parent (Watson 1984; Watson and Fischer 1980). Children play these relationships before they can describe or explain them (McLoyd, Warren, and Thomas 1984; Rubin and Howe 1986). Decentration is pushed toward its upper limits as children contend with the complexities of pretend roles and the identities of play partners.

Eventually, children will understand that they can simultaneously be a mother, a daughter, a sister, and a friend. Furthermore, they will understand that different behaviors, privileges, and responsibilities go with these different roles. The great and important insight is that a constant, stable self can participate in many different relational systems. At four years of age, this emerging understanding is exercised in pretend play. At six or seven, children will be able to think about and discuss these ideas in nonplay contexts (Watson 1984).

INTERPERSONAL COMPETENCE

In Cycle I, Camille reminds Kevin of a pretend game they had played before. She calls the creature a "worm" perhaps because she really doesn't know that a "bloodsucker" is a kind of leech, slimy like a worm, but in other respects quite different.

Kevin knows what she means. He doesn't correct her, but immediately asserts the presence of *his* pretend creatures, adding another creature, a spider. Camille doesn't argue with his substitution of a bloodsucker for a worm, but she pointedly confirms the presence of a spider, increasing its significance by making it a big spider. In this incredibly brief exchange, these children manage a complex negotiation about the nature of pretend entities, with each child granting to the other the right to impose a personal perspective upon a collective construction (Fein 1989; Goncu 1987).

In social pretending children communicate what they are doing or planning to do. Because the persons or things represented in the play are not actually present and crucial events never actually happened, children must inform their partners about the status of an episode if the partners are to participate. Children as young as three seem to recognize this social necessity. Between ages three and six, they elaborate a complex communication system for sharing pretend information with one another. They use special communicative techniques or metacommunications to talk about what they will talk about in the play (Bateson 1955; Giffin 1984). Some metacommunicative messages are easy to detect. When a child says, "Let's pretend . . . ," it is apparent that the child is referring to a pretend episode that might occur soon in the future. But "in-play," "out-of-play," and "about-play" messages differ in other ways as well (Pellegrini 1986). For example, children use the past tense to give stage directions: "We were in the boat and the sharks came." But they use the present tense to enact the play: "There's two bloodsuckers and a spider in this boat." The language used in pretend is more complex, connected, and cohesive than that used in other play and nonplay settings (Garvey and Kramer 1989; Pellegrini 1986). When children engage in pretend, they display language functions and linguistic forms that are more advanced than their speech in other contexts. Again, pretend play encourages children to function at the upper levels of their developmental capabilities.

SOCIAL AND PHYSICAL KNOWLEDGE

Camille proposes swords to battle bloodsuckers and spiders. An adult might say that a sword is an excessively harsh weapon to combat such small creatures. The weapons we choose to combat those who threaten us often exceed the actual threat these people present. Human beings, even adults, have enormous difficulty managing fine distinctions between perceived and actual threat, between small and big threat. In schools, these issues are addressed in social studies, history, or political science. Should the teacher intervene to suggest that bloodsuckers and spiders can be combated with milder means? Because the adult did not intervene, we can examine the children's own solutions to the more general problem of threat and counterthreat.

Cycle I concluded when the children returned to the boat after having demolished the creatures with pretend swords. The creatures are reproduced in Cycle II. But Camille proposes a dramatically different solution: avoid the creatures by getting out of their way. Kevin and the other children ignore her proposal. Yale, still preoccupied with the notion of high threat, calls upon the superhero symbol of He-Man and Kevin exploits this idea choosing a superhero known for his terrible sword. Kevin thus maintains symbolic continuity with Cycle I. Both children evoke symbols of superhuman power, as if these symbols reinforce their capacity to overcome threatening creatures. Once reassured, Kevin is able in Cycle III to put a bloodsucker on Camille's shoe and simply brush it away with his hand. A mild solution to a mild threat comes about after powerful symbols of strength and competence are evoked.

One can think of this episode as a child-generated social studies lesson. An observant teacher might ask about the play during group time. Perhaps a curriculum unit on problems of threat and counterthreat might help the children to elaborate and refine their implicit knowledge of conflict and conflict resolution. The episode touches scientific matters as well. What are spiders? Bloodsuckers? Crocodiles? Sharks? In this play, the children classify these creatures. Camille may not know what a bloodsucker is. Does Kevin know how a worm and a bloodsucker differ? Probably not. In social pretend children share what they find interesting, and responsive teachers can build upon the clues and themes that emerge.

TEACHING FROM PLAY

Some play theorists concentrate on the knowledge children bring *to* their play; these theorists view play as a script derived from established knowledge (Bretherton 1984; 1989). For script theorists, play reveals what children know. Other theorists stress the knowledge children take *from* their play; for these theorists the knowledge brought to play is fuzzy, but interesting (Fein and Apfel 1979). For "fuzzy knowledge" theorists, play reveals what children are curious about; it is emergent knowledge at the upper reaches of the ZPD.

A teacher who subscribes to the fuzzy knowledge perspective will wonder what the children know about the creatures represented in the play. To find out, it will be necessary to find other opportunities to probe their understanding. A teacher who is aware of what children are pretending can build a unit of study from their interests and concerns. Camille and Kevin's teacher might use their interests to design a unit about big and small creatures, slimy creatures, or creepy creatures.

Pretend play offers young children an opportunity to express their understanding, interests, and concerns. This play is consistent with a rich cultural curriculum built from what children bring to the classroom as well as what teachers bring to the children. It requires children to use sophisticated symbolic transformations, linguistic forms, and social strategies. Social pretend brings natural symbolic forms into the classroom. Formal academic skills acquire meaning and urgency when they are taught in the context of culture and expression. The issue *need not* be cast as alternatives: as *either* academic *or* playful activities. Rather, playful activities, storytelling, story reading, drawing, and painting, embedded in an imaginative cultural curriculum, evoke and extend core symbolic competencies without which academic proficiencies cannot be attained.

REFERENCES

Bateson, G. 1955. A Theory of Play and Fantasy. *Psychiatric Research Reports* 2: 39–51.

Belsky, J., and Most, R. K. 1981. From Exploration to Play: A Cross-Sectional Study of Infant Free Play Behavior. *Developmental Psychology* 17: 630–39.

Bretherton, I. 1984. Representing the Social World in Symbolic Play: Reality and Fantasy. In *Symbolic Play: The Development of Social Understanding,* edited by I. Bretherton, 3–41. New York: Academic Press.

———. 1989. Pretense: The Form and Function of Make-Believe Play. *Developmental Review* 9: 383–401.

Fein, G. G. 1975. A Transformational Analysis of Pretending. *Developmental Psychology* 11: 291–96.

———. 1981. Pretend Play: An Integrative Review. *Child Development* 52: 1095–1118.

———. 1989. Mind, Meaning, and Affect: Proposals for a Theory of Pretense. *Developmental Review* 9: 345–63.

Fein, G. G., and Apfel, N. 1979. Some Preliminary Observations on Knowing and Pretending. In *Symbolic Functioning in Childhood,* edited by N. Smith and M. Franklin, 87–100. Hillsdale, N.J.: Erlbaum.

Fein, G. G., and Schwartz, S. S. 1986. The Social Coordination of Pretense in Preschool Children. In *The Young Child at Play: Reviews of Research,* vol. 4, edited by G. G. Fein and M. S. Rivkin, 95–112. Washington, D.C.: National Association for the Education of Young Children.

Garvey, C., and Kramer, T. L. 1989. The Language of Social Pretend Play. *Developmental Review* 9: 364–82.

Giffin, H. 1984. The Coordination of Meaning in the Creation of Shared Make-Believe Reality. In *Symbolic Play: The Development of*

Social Understanding, edited by I. Bretherton, 73–101. New York: Academic Press.

Goncu, A. 1987. Toward an Interactional Model of Developmental Changes in Social Pretend Play. In *Current Topics in Early Childhood Education,* vol. 7, edited by L. Katz, 108–25. Norwood, N.J.: Ablex.

Matthews, W. S. 1977. Modes of Transformation in the Initiation of Fantasy Play. *Developmental Psychology* 13: 212–16.

McLoyd, V. C.; Warren, D.; and Thomas, E. A. C. 1984. Anticipatory and Fantastic Role Enactment in Preschool Triads. *Developmental Psychology* 20: 807–14.

Mead, G. H. 1934. *Mind, Self, and Society.* Chicago: University of Chicago Press.

Nicolich, L. 1977. Beyond Sensorimotor Intelligence: Measurement of Symbolic Maturity Through Analysis of Pretend Play. *Merrill-Palmer Quarterly* 23: 89–99.

Pellegrini, A. 1986. Communicating in and about Play: The Effect of Play Centers on Preschoolers' Explicit Language. In *The Young Child at Play: Reviews of Research,* vol. 4, edited by G. G. Fein and M. S. Rivkin, 79–92. Washington, D.C.: National Association for the Education of Young Children.

————. 1988. Elementary School Children's Rough-and-Tumble Play and Social Competence. *Developmental Psychology* 24: 802–6.

Piaget, J. 1962. *Play, Dreams and Imitation in Childhood.* New York: Norton.

Rubin, K.; Fein, G. G.; and Vandenberg, B. 1983. Play. In *Handbook of Child Psychology, Vol. 4. Socialization, Personality and Social Development,* edited by P. H. Mussen and E. M. Hetherington, 693–774. New York: Wiley.

Vygotsky, L. S. 1967. Play and Its Role in the Mental Development of the Child. *Soviet Psychology* 5: 6–18.

Watson, M. W. 1984. Development of Social Role Understanding. *Developmental Review* 4: 192–213.

Watson, M. W., and Fischer, K. W. 1980. Development of Social Roles in Elicited and Spontaneous Behavior During the Preschool Years. *Developmental Psychology* 16: 483–94.

Chapter 3

FOUR- AND FIVE-YEAR-OLDS: INTUITIVE, IMAGINATIVE PLAYERS

by Nancy E. Curry

SCENARIO: OH, THOSE FRUSTRATING FOURS AND FIVES!

Teachers who encounter four-year-olds for the first time may be intrigued by their imaginativeness, dismayed by their high activity level, suspicious of their limit-testing capacities, and overly zealous in their expectations. Consider the following:

Joey, a four-year-old, gets up cheerily from his afternoon nap. He needed the rest after a busy morning of building an elaborate racetrack for his and his friends' version of Demolition Derby, playing out a complicated scenario involving Teenage Mutant Ninja Turtles in between bouts of puzzles, and making multicolored monsters at the easel. The afternoon staff has changed and for the next hour Joey is swept up in a series of teacher-directed activities: an assigned art project making Halloween pumpkins, a Halloween story, finger plays, a simple game requiring the finding of different colors throughout the room, and learning the words to a new song. Initially, he is attentive and eager to respond to the teacher's directives. Throughout the story, his questions and comments are pertinent and show a good grasp of the content. But soon he begins to fidget, then tickles his friend, has a "foot fight" with another friend, and finally gets sent to the time out chair, from which he darts, when released, to the craft table, where he defiantly sweeps all the materials onto the floor. More time out is used, and he dissolves into noisy tears that escalate into a tantrum when he is isolated in the locker area until he is "ready to be a part of the group." When his father arrives to pick him up, he finds his son tear-stained and grouchy. The teacher rolls her eyes at his father and wearily says, "He's had a typical four-year-old day"—cold comfort to the father who now takes him home to two exhausted parents and a baby sister, also reverberating from her day in care.

Is this a typical day for a four-year-old? Most potential teachers unused to this age group would shudder at the behavior described and think how they might handle the situation—from calling the parents in for a conference on their "unmanageable" child, to deciding to curtail the amount of time he spends in aggressive play in the morning, to devising a system of rewards and punishments to deal with his behavior next time, to deciding he is too immature for the program and recommending a transfer to a younger group, to assigning him to a place closer to the teacher so she can restrain him physically if necessary.

What we know about the way children grow and develop, however, tells us that this *is* four-year-old behavior, and the responsibility for effectively guiding and teaching this child must be placed on the program, not the small boy, since we know that

1. Four- and five-year-olds are exceedingly curious and hungry to learn.
2. They are as eager to please their teachers and parents as they are to defy them.
3. They are enthusiastic participants in group activities for short (brief) periods of time.
4. They express strong feelings when they feel they are treated unfairly.
5. They have an abundance of energy and the physical capacities to try out all sorts of motor skills.
6. They have an upsurge of aggressive energy that sometimes leads to physical and verbal brawls, but when channeled can lead to productive and creative activities.
7. They are intent upon and expert in developing peer relationships that at times take precedence over relationships with beloved adults.

8. Most of all, they are intense, goal-directed players who can use play to both demonstrate and enhance their physical, emotional, social, and cognitive development.

This chapter will focus on the importance of play for developing four- and five-year-olds, recognizing that most practicing teachers may have had more experience with older children and thus tend to either over- or underestimate the capacities of this intriguing age group.

THE PLAY OF FOUR- AND FIVE-YEAR-OLDS

Most authors are in agreement with Piaget's classification of play into sensorimotor, constructive, symbolic, and games-with-rules (Fein 1981). Sutton-Smith (1972) uses another set of descriptive labels for the different types of play: imitation, exploration, testing, and world construction. He talks of these as ways children use to know about their worlds.

While all these forms of play are seen in four- and five-year-olds' classes, it does appear that *pretend or symbolic play* increases markedly during these years, if the setting permits it, and causes great delight in observers of these play groups. Paley's books, especially *Bad Guys Don't Have Birthdays* (1988) and *Boys and Girls: Superheroes in the Doll Corner* (1984), give masterful word pictures of the play lives of children in these age groups. Preschool teachers and play-invested parents can attest to the richness of such preschool play.

Sensorimotor Play

This label describes play in which children use their physical capacities to discover and explore every aspect of their world, both human and nonhuman. Thus, a baby touches, tastes, gazes at, and listens to any available object in her environment, often in very playful encounters. At a more sophisticated level, late preschoolers do the same. Although sensorimotor play is listed developmentally as the earliest form of play, Rubin, Fein, and Vandenberg (1983) noted that it accounts for about 33 percent of all free activities by age five. At this age such play also includes *testing* (Sutton-Smith 1972); late preschoolers spend much of their time testing their body competence through climbing, running, pulling, pushing, hopping, slithering through tunnels, sliding down inclines, and riding vehicles. In a 45-minute observation I conducted of a four-year-old, he spent the entire time at the neighborhood park with his parents and two siblings testing himself on every possible piece of equipment with all these motor variations before challenging his father to an impromptu soccer game (thus demonstrating how sensorimotor play links up with games with rules).

Most four-year-olds now focus as much, if not more, on the product as they do on the process of play. But the sensory nature of plastic and fluid materials and the motor aspects of wheel toys may invite children to get bogged down in sensorimotor exploration rather than in their constructive or representational possibilities. In her studies of the differences between exploration and play, Hutt (1971) found that when confronted with new toys or materials, children first needed to spend time exploring all their properties before they could engage in dramatic play. Thus, children critically need more than just the few minutes of obligatory "free play" so often assigned to times of transition, such as early morning entry, after story, and during cleanup for lunch, or after the afternoon nap as they wait to be picked up by their parents. Children need time to engage in sensorimotor and exploratory activities that help them learn about their world, but also as warm-up to the symbolic play so useful as a foundation for school-related tasks (Klugman and Smilansky 1990).

Those of us who consult in programs for disadvantaged young children are struck with the predominance of sensorimotor play, as if the children are "stuck" in a mode of play that is not enhancing their symbolic capacities. These children especially need adult facilitation to progress to a more symbolic play mode. (See Smilansky and Shefatya 1990.)

Constructive Play

In this play children "manipulate objects to construct or create something" (Monighan-Nourot, Scales, Van Hoorn, and Almy 1987, 26). Constructive play takes up 51 percent of children's free activities at ages four, five, and six (Rubin et al. 1983). Thus, the late preschooler is capable of building elaborate block buildings; making interesting constructions at the woodworking table; designing intriguing art projects from scraps, cardboard, and other collage materials; and even arranging and rearranging the classroom furniture. Sutton-Smith (1972) would probably include this type of play under *imitation,* for children seem to be trying to model their constructions on the known. At the same time they are also creating something uniquely their own, and in the process, increasing their competence (Forman and Hill 1980).

For these constructive activities, children again need time, well-placed materials presented with clarity and accessibility, and the teacher's permission—sometimes even assistance—to use the materials in a variety of ways (Curry and Arnaud 1984). Many teachers restrict children transporting materials from one center to another—for example, when completion of a castle in the block corner may need the ornamentation only a set of parquet blocks from the puzzle corner can provide.

Dramatic Play

This type of play has been greatly researched in the past 20 years because of its potential for enhancing many aspects of development necessary for later school success. (See Fein 1981; and Rubin, Fein, and Vandenberg 1983, for comprehensive reviews of this research.) Some authors refer to it as pretend play, symbolic play, fantasy play, or as role enactment; Sutton-Smith (1972) calls it *world construction.*

Smilansky and Shefatya (1990) have given the clearest definition through clarifying the elements necessary for dramatic play:

1. Imitative role play—"I'm the mailman."
2. Make-believe in regard to objects—"I'll use these blocks for the letters."
3. Make-believe in regard to actions and situations—"Pretend a dog chased me and now I don't bring any more mail."
4. Persistence. The play episode lasts for at least ten minutes.

To qualify as sociodramatic play, these researchers add the following two elements:

5. Interaction, involving at least two players—"Now you be the mailman and I'll be the dog."
6. Verbal communication—"Let's tell the customers that the dog has to be in the doghouse and then you'll deliver the mail."

Having achieved a sense of self/other constancy in the first three years of life, the four- and five-year-olds play out their perceptions of that self and their perceptions of others through in-depth dramatic play roles (Curry 1986; Fein 1984; Curry and Johnson 1990). With a firmer sense of self, late preschoolers are fascinated by the wide variety of people who touch their lives, either in actuality or in stories or on television. They have a heightened interest in romance and in the current powerful folk heroes (Ghostbusters, Teenage Mutant Ninja Turtles). They realize that there is much to be known about the world that can be scary and unfathomable at times; they symbolize their awe through heightened interest in dinosaurs and monsters and other "supernatural" beings.

The *style* and *theme* of children's play can tell us much about how they view themselves. Gould (1972) has given us a way of evaluating children's play. Her premise is that children depict their primary experiences with care giving through their play styles and themes. Four- and five-year-old children who have been well nurtured can maintain a steady stance of pretend, have a sense of entitlement, know the difference between real and pretend, and predominantly play the roles of nurturer and provider (e.g., all superheroes have a protective side). Children who have been treated aggressively have difficulty in sustaining a role, have a sense of "global self-condemnation," confuse reality with pretense, and have a primary identification with the aggressor or victim, thus playing out their early experience with punitive or neglectful care giving.

The elements that Smilansky and Shefatya (1990) have used to define both dramatic and sociodramatic play should be present in the play of four- and five-year-olds. Further, their play contains:

1. A move from dyadic (mother/baby, doctor/patient, daddy animal/baby animal) to triadic roles (mother/father/baby, doctor/nurse/patient, brother/sister/family pet). Parents are portrayed not just as care givers but also as people who have lives outside the home and multiple roles in society.

2. A clear depiction of the full essence of the role, which portrays not only the physical aspects of the person (the elegant lady with veils, scarves, jewelry, high heels, and a briefcase), but also the emotional attributes of the person (e.g., the distraught zookeeper who must cope with a herd of runaway monkeys).

3. The need for the external trappings of the role with emphasis on the ultramasculine and ultrafeminine. The dress-up corner needs all the festoonings of femininity, as well as male clothing that can be used for all sorts of aggrandized male roles, including superheroes (the bane of teachers' existence). These give children opportunities to try out their perceptions of the powerful adults around them.

4. Numerous opportunities to use other symbolic channels, such as art (crayons, cardboard carton sculptures, markers, easel paints, collage materials, chalk, fingerpaint), music (tapes and records for

eurythmics), large and small blocks, puppets, and sand and water tables, as well as miniature life toys to permit children to create dramas one step removed from enacting the role themselves.

5. The capacity and interest to play out their perceptions of the roles of anyone with whom they come into contact in real life (e.g., fire and police personnel, bosses, librarians, truck drivers, transplant surgeons), and via television and stories (e.g., kings, queens, "The Brady Bunch," astronauts, cowboys, *Rainbow Brite*). (See Arnaud 1972; Curry and Arnaud 1974; and Curry and Bergen 1987 for further explication of this material.)

6. Games with rules. While fours and fives are notoriously poor losers and blatant cheaters in competitive board games and organized group games, they relish making up their own games with rules that can be arbitrary and inalterable one moment and muddled or overturned the next. It is as if they are fascinated by rules that lure them to break them, both in play and reality. They also condemn children who break unspoken rules (one kindergartner playing mother to a group of fractious three-year-olds broke out of her role to chide one bumptious little boy, "You *never* hit mothers!"). Creating their own racing and chasing games introduces them to tolerable competition. Smilansky and Shefatya (1990) postulated that most superhero play really should be categorized as games-with-rules, since many children seem driven to play out unvarying scenarios that appear rule-bound.

Play described in this chapter is within the repertoire of four- and five-year-olds only IF it is facilitated by an environment that is rich in carefully chosen and well-maintained materials and by adults who are convinced that such play is vital for optimal learning strategies, such as decentration, reversibility, problem solving, creativity, and empathy. With such a play curriculum, children are able to become increasingly self-directed and intrinsically motivated, and they experience more positive affect concerning school—all attributes espoused for effective learners.

REVISED SCENARIO:
OH, THOSE FANTASTIC FOURS AND FIVES!

Joey gets up cheerily from his afternoon nap. While drinking some juice and eating a hard-cooked egg, he and his cohorts plan a continuation of their morning block play. Then he joins the teacher who is reading a Halloween story and responds appropriately and with excitement to the unfolding drama. When she has finished the story and has sung a Halloween song with suitable hand motions, she asks the children to choose what they would like to do. To carry out the holiday theme, the craft table has small real pumpkins with markers available to make faces as jack-o'-lanterns. Another teacher is playing the piano and encouraging the children to make up motions that suit the music. The teacher has saved the racetrack in the block area that Joey and his friends used so intently that morning.

Joey calls to his friends to resume the Demolition Derby game, but they decide to call it a Spook Train. They decide to make tickets to sell to those who want to take a ride. They carefully cut out rectangular pieces of paper, mark them with dollar signs and numbers, and call out to other children, "Who wants to buy tickets?" A couple of takers buy tickets, but then they join the building and want to crash the cars. Joey complains to the teacher that they are being taken over by the ticket buyers. She points out the need for block buildings to serve as refreshment stands at their train site and Joey picks up the idea with enthusiasm. He even decides to make signs for the stands, asking the teacher's help to spell the words so he can write the letters he knows. The block corner grows noisy, but the sound is purposeful and the children are intent on their project. Some parents begin to pick up their children. Joey asks the teacher if they can keep their structures up, and she helps him make a sign: "Please Save."

45

When Joey looks tired, the teacher suggests that he draw a face on his pumpkin; he does a fair imitation of a turtle face. Resting his head on the table, he hums to the piano music. The teacher asks if he'd like to sit on the bench beside her and he gets up eagerly, nestles at her side, and sings the words to a favorite folk song. When Joey's father arrives, he comments on the peaceful scene. Roused, his son races across the room and slides into his father's legs like a baseball player hitting home plate. Joey proudly shows his dad his block structure with the sign, saying, "We're going to add a hideout tomorrow!" and points out his Ninja Turtle pumpkin face, and the two leave companionably.

REFERENCES

Arnaud, S. H. 1972. Polish for Play's Tarnished Reputation. In *Play: The Child Strives Toward Self-Realization,* edited by G. Engstrom, 5–12. Washington, D.C.: National Association for the Education of Young Children.

Curry, N. E. 1986. Where Have All the Players Gone? In *The Feeling Child: Affective Development Reconsidered,* edited by N. E. Curry. New York: Haworth.

Curry, N. E., and Arnaud, S. H. 1974. Cognitive Implications in Children's Spontaneous Role Play. *Theory into Practice* 13, no. 4: 273–77.

———. 1984. Play in Developmental Preschool Settings. In *Child's Play: Developmental and Applied,* edited by T. D. Yawkey and A. D. Pellegrini, 273–90. Hillsdale, N.J.: Erlbaum.

Curry, N. E., and Bergen, D. 1987. The Relationship of Play to Emotional, Social, and Gender/Sex Role Development. In *Play as a Medium for Learning and Development,* edited by D. Bergen, 107–31. Portsmouth, N.H.: Heinemann.

Curry, N. E., and Johnson, C. N. 1990. *Beyond Self-Esteem: Developing a Genuine Sense of Human Value.* Washington, D.C.: National Association for the Education of Young Children.

Fein, G. G. 1981. Pretend Play: An Integrative Review. *Child Development* 52: 1095–1118.

———. 1984. The Self-Building Potential of Preschool Play in "I

Got a Fish All by Myself." In *Child's Play: Developmental and Applied,* edited by T. D. Yawkey and A. D. Pellegrini. Hillsdale, N.J.: Erlbaum.

Forman, G. E., and Hill, F. 1980. *Constructive Play: Applying Piaget in the Classroom.* Monterey, Calif.: Brooks/Cole.

Gould, R. 1972. *Child Studies Through Fantasy.* New York: Quadrangle.

Hutt, C. 1971. Exploration and Play in Children. In *Child's Play,* edited by R. E. Herron and B. Sutton-Smith, 231–51. New York: Wiley.

Klugman, E., and Smilansky, S., eds. 1990. *Children's Play and Learning: Perspectives and Policy Implications.* New York: Teachers College Press.

Monighan-Nourot, P.; Scales, B.; Van Hoorn, J.; and Almy, M. 1987. *Looking at Children's Play: The Bridge from Theory to Practice.* New York: Teachers College Press.

Paley, V. G. 1984. *Boys and Girls: Superheroes in the Doll Corner.* Chicago: University of Chicago Press.

———. 1988. *Bad Guys Don't Have Birthdays: Fantasy Play at Four.* Chicago: University of Chicago Press.

Rubin, K.; Fein, G.; and Vandenberg, B. 1983. Play. In *Handbook of Child Psychology, Vol. 4. Socialization, Personality and Social Development,* edited by P. H. Mussen and E. M. Hetherington, 693–774. New York: Wiley.

Smilansky, S., and Shefatya, L. 1990. *Facilitating Play: A Medium for Promoting Cognitive, Social-Emotional and Academic Development in Young Children.* Gaithersburg, Md.: Psychosocial and Educational Publications.

Sutton-Smith, B. 1972. The Playful Ways of Knowing. In *Play: The Child Strives Toward Self-Realization,* edited by G. Engstrom, 13–25. Washington, D.C.: National Association for the Education of Young Children.

Chapter 4

IN THE BEST INTEREST OF CHILDREN: RETURNING PLAY TO ITS PLACE

by Mary Ellen Sapp

More than 30 years ago, Laura Zirbes, a noted educator whose mission was to "spur creative teaching," contrasted two approaches to early education. She came close to describing the controversy in public school kindergarten and primary education today. Zirbes' (1959) depiction can be used as a checklist to determine which elements exist in today's kindergartens and first grades:

[Creative]

A group of young children manifests spontaneity and individuality when it is not regimented or repressed by imposed restraints and required conformity. Provided with challenging opportunities to explore and discover the possibilities of a variety of play materials, these children have a chance to move about, to handle things, to act on impulse, to react to each other, and to the situation. They manifest freedom to communicate, freedom to be spontaneously playful, as well as freedom to initiate purposeful endeavor. There is no sign of pressures which block or inhibit action or pressures which are coercive.

[Uncreative]

In sharp contrast with this situation another group of children of the same age range is provided with uniform, stereotyped seatwork, and explicit oral directions to be followed in varying compliance. These children sit in rather passive, compliant preoccupation with this task without noting much else, and without having anything to do with each other. The situation is clearly one in which an efficient type of mass management has everything in control to an extent which discourages deviation from directions. Any thought of individual initiative would seem to be too precarious to occur to children. This accounts for anxiously submissive adaptation, and also for lack of zest. The room is very quiet and there is nothing dynamic or challenging to spur children to go beyond what they are required to do, without choice or variation or adjustment of expectations in terms of evident differences in maturity or capacity. There is no evidence of intrinsic satisfaction—no enthusiasm. (pp. 21–22)

While the National Association for the Education of Young Children calls for developmentally appropriate practices (Bredekamp 1987) matching Zirbes' preferred creative learning, many schools continue to provide a drill-and-practice workbook approach to learning that does not consider individual differences. A need for organizational efficiency and a failure to understand and apply sound principles of child development are two reasons for uncreative learning in the primary grades (Doremus 1986).

A developmentally appropriate program incorporates play, enabling young children to be in control, to continue an activity because of intrinsic motivation, and to use their imaginations (Neumann, cited in Ellis 1973). Teachers of young children should be engineers of the kinds of learning that evolve when they maximize play potential in their classrooms.

As part of the school reform movement, states are passing legislation that dictates prescribed amounts of time for instruction in subject areas and sets specific goals and objectives, with the same standards for all young children. Teachers are in the middle—pressured for achievement that is measurable by standardized tests, yet urged to "take back their curriculum and resist conforming to practices that they believe are not in the best interest of children" (Freeman 1990, 33).

This chapter presents the stories of four kindergarten and first grade teachers, risk-takers who are "taking back their

50

curriculum" to meet the developmental needs of the children they teach, and one school administrator who led curriculum reform within his school serving young children. In these examples, *teachers had the support and approval of their building administrators, a necessary first step in making curricular change.* These examples also emphasize the importance of the following:

1. Teachers of young children being able to explain the value of play
2. Administrators and supervisors understanding and affirming the value of play
3. Basing decisions about the education of young children on more than one test
4. Ongoing in-service education for teachers moving to a developmentally appropriate curriculum
5. Involving parents in planning for a developmentally appropriate curriculum.

EXPLAINING THE VALUE OF PLAY

Harriet Babcock (1986), a teacher on the west coast of Florida with a playful approach to life, was asked by her principal to change teaching assignments and to implement a new approach in kindergarten based on her strong background in early childhood education and her teaching experience. She recalls that "the kindergarten's impoverished physical setting and traditional expectations, such as kindergarten graduation, generated considerable opportunity for inventiveness" (p. 3). And invent she did! She inherited "a 1935 upright piano, 3 child size work tables with 24 stack'em chairs, a child size cupboard and stove, wooden blocks, a few puzzles, 6 pegboards and a handful of pegs" (p. 6). Although the school budget provided ample funds for workbooks, no money was available for the materials Babcock needed.

Babcock's goal was to provide extensive language experience and to promote cognitive development through sociodramatic play, an approach she knew did not align with the back-to-basics movement. Through her understanding of the work of Smilansky (1968), *she was able to explain the value of play*, to gain support, and to convince administrators as well as parents that she needed kindergarten play materials. Dolls, telephones, table blocks, dinosaurs, and tricycles were the first additions, some from the school storage closet. Fund-raisers provided monies for purchases of other materials that could be used in open-ended activities: "boxes, sheets, paper, paper cups, glue, string, fish nets, rulers, nails and hammers, 2 x 4 and 2 x 2 boards, pencils, paint, yarn, sticks, playing cards, spot light, flour, and old magazines" (Babcock 1986, 18).

Following Smilansky's guidelines, Babcock set up sociodramatic play areas of which the most successful in extending play themes was "the veterinarian." Children brought stuffed animals from home, and Babcock used this opportunity to introduce the care of pets. A veterinarian visited the class, talked about the care of pets, and demonstrated how she examined animals. That afternoon, Babcock and the children rearranged the classroom and made a small area into the veterinarian's office. She describes the office setting as including "a waiting room with two chairs, a telephone, pads of paper, pencils, a stethoscope, a desk converted to examining table, surgeon's scrubs and nurse's apparel, a play medical kit, small discarded medicine bottles, bandages, and boxes converted to cages" (p. 20). Babcock intervened to extend play, claiming that "it was natural for the children to invite the teacher to play . . . as *the teacher was the primary source of stimulation*" (p. 18). She "modeled several roles . . . developed and encouraged dialogue, used symbolic and genuine props in the activities, and assisted children in role selection, rearranging furniture, and making additional props" (p. 25).

Babcock compared audiotape recordings of play sessions to evaluate language development. Her analysis indicated that initial sociodramatic play before teacher intervention in the veterinarian's office included children giving orders to others, such as "I'm going to be the doctor. You be the dog!" (p. 30), requests and threats, and much questioning. "Commands such as, 'You, you give me that!' and primitive arguments" (p. 30) abounded. Evaluation of the tapes following the teacher's intervention indicated that:

> *Most children had chosen or been given roles, selected props, and could participate together in a positive manner, exchanging props, accepting others' ideas. The children engaged in play themes after brief quarrels (about 14 seconds) on what to do and made rapid role changes and transformations of objects. Answers were given to unasked questions, "Yeah," [holding a toy horse], "he ate too much hay." (Babcock 1986, 30)*

Although teachers may say that they value play, they usually cannot explain its educational potential. Babcock's ability to explain the value of play came from her background in early childhood education and child growth and development. *Teachers of young children should have degrees in early childhood education.*

Babcock's comment that she was "the primary source of stimulation" (1986, 18) is a factor deemed vital by Ellis (1973), who calls for the adult to be "the most complex and interesting object" (p. 131) in the play situation. Play, according to Ellis, does not teach specific responses but is preparation for successfully encountering the unknown. He says the teacher's role is to "maximize the playfulness of a setting" (p. 124).

UNDERSTANDING AND AFFIRMING THE VALUE OF PLAY

While Harriet Babcock's new kindergarten approach was initiated by her principal, Mary Dickerson (1989) had a different school climate. Dickerson, a kindergarten teacher in Georgia, decided to move from having all children participate in the same task at the same time to a curriculum that used learning centers, yet remained within state and local guidelines that prescribed schedules, curriculum, and specific goals and objectives. Dickerson believes that "each child needs to learn differently and that

53

each child needs to learn at his/her own pace. . . . but knowing what was best for children and being able to do what was best is not always easy" (p. 7).

The advice that helped her most when she began to establish centers came from McCabe (1978), who cautioned teachers trying learning centers for the first time to establish only a few centers. Because she needed to demonstrate to administrators her students' specific skills, Dickerson set up a folder for each child and trained her aide to observe children, to record data on the checklists she created, and to function as a facilitator with children (an ongoing task for her). *Teacher-directed learning is a difficult habit to change.*

The easiest center for Dickerson to set up was one on nutrition that met all state and local guidelines for content, yet involved the children in decision making, problem solving, and classifying. While the center might be classified as work disguised as play (Sponseller 1974), it represents a positive move away from a seatwork, ditto approach.

> *In the nutrition center each child was asked to get pictures from home of the four different food groups. . . . an effort to involve the parents . . . my aide and I also brought in pictures that were placed in a basket so children could decide themselves into which group pictures were to be placed in booklets that they created. Children used paper plates to make a balanced meal using the food pictures. They also analyzed the school lunchroom food to determine if they could identify the four food groups. (Dickerson 1989, 16–17)*

At the end of the 12-week project, Dickerson reported that children achieved mastery of required skills through participation in a learning center. She demonstrated to her supervisors that learning center content correlated with mandated objectives.

EDUCATIONAL DECISIONS AND TESTS

Working with 16 south Florida kindergartners whose

readiness test scores placed them at risk for kindergarten success, Raquel Kubala (1989) decided to move from using a structured language development kit to implementation of an activity-oriented program that included semantic mapping (Heimlich and Pittelman 1986; Stahl and Vancil 1986), storytelling, creative dramatics, experiential learning, and elements of the language experience approach. She initiated a 12-week program using children's literature as the foundation. A different book was selected weekly with semantic mapping as the opening activity. Children brainstormed words related to the title and theme of the book, and then listened to the story and added to their maps. Creative dramatics was the third step in Kubala's program, with kindergartners acting out the story and adding their own interpretations. Cooking and field trips extended the ideas gleaned from the stories. Children dictated stories and experiences as a final step in the process.

Kubala provided free-play time each day for her kindergartners, during which she observed children moving naturally from guided creative dramatics to self-initiated sociodramatic play. After reading *The Story of Ferdinand* to the children, she added artifacts from Spain to the classroom. During free play the matador's cape became a prop for sociodramatic play, as did the castanets, with play themes involving girls as dancers. Following *Stone Soup*, the role of soldier became part of sociodramatic play. *Madeline* introduced hospital concepts that interested the children so much that Kubala invited the school nurse to visit the classroom as a resource person. Children listened to each other's heartbeat with the stethoscope. Sociodramatic play took on new themes as nurses and doctors cared for sick patients (sometimes soldiers or bullfighters), fed them *Chicken Soup with Rice*, and covered the sick with the cape.

Evaluating children's progress through analyses of the semantic maps, the language experience stories dictated by the children, and the audiotape recordings of language samples, Kubala found increases in language development that surpassed her expectations. Records indicated that children persisted as long as one hour in storytelling and related activities. Changes occurred in self-initiated free-time activities, including chanting, retelling of stories, making masks, continuing the creative dramatics, adding new endings to stories, and beginning sociodramatic play where none had existed before the project. While creative dramatics does not have the play potential of sociodramatic play because the degree of spontaneity and improvisation is diminished and roles and plots stay the same (Smilansky and Shefatya 1990), Kubala's children developed skills in sequencing, immediate recall, categorizing, logical thinking, and cause-and-effect relationships. Kubala introduced *a number of methods for measuring children's growth in language development rather than depending on one sample gleaned from a standardized, group test.*

IN-SERVICE EDUCATION

Miranti Murphy (1990) took a leadership role at her south Florida elementary school, where she assisted first grade teachers in their move from a workbook-oriented, rote-memorization-and-drill mathematics program to an approach that developed problem-solving and critical thinking skills, areas that the school's self-study had identified as needing improvement. Murphy's goal was to provide exploratory learning to develop skills in brainstorming, interactive and cooperative learning, and deductive reasoning.

Before Murphy's project, "teachers had provided unchallenging mathematics lessons by restricting discussions, prohibiting student interactions, and reaching conclusions without explanations of processes" (1990, 46). As teachers made greater use of manipulatives, interactions, and real-life applications in teaching mathematical concepts, the self-confidence of teachers and children increased. Sociograms kept during the project indicated that all first graders became interactive in math activities.

Ideas for Murphy's project came, in part, from Henniger (1987), who stated that by using discovery, exploration, and discussion, children would develop a curiosity for mathematics deemed vital for building mathematical skills during their lifetimes. Through the introduction of interpretive discussions and real-life applications (Baroody 1989), Murphy laid the foundation for symbolic thinking skills. She describes the first attempts at moving to the use of manipulatives and group discussions during math time as follows:

> At first, students were uncooperative and competitive. For example, students often argued about who had correct answers and did not listen to the point of view of others. However, students soon began to interact positively as their teachers encouraged brainstorming activities and differing points of view. Thus, students worked in teams and interacted productively as they became more cooperative, attentive, and collaborative. The mathematical themes implemented included: numbers, sets, geometry, time, monetary values, measurement, operations, and logical thinking. (Murphy 1990, 33)

Murphy says first graders moved from workbooks to guided learning with manipulatives, to discovery learning and problem solving. Table games with rules involving counting and computation were added to the activities. Play themes developed around money, measurement, and buying and selling.

Murphy used anecdotal records, observed students and teachers, and examined sociograms to chart cognitive and interactive growth during her project. As she was also faced with school district objectives for mastery, Murphy concluded that the children had exceeded mandated expectations with her approach.

PARENTAL INVOLVEMENT AND PLANNING

John R. Currie (1990), principal of the new Seminole Springs Elementary School in Eustis, Florida, envisioned his school moving to an upgraded primary concept for kindergarten through second grade. To bring about the changes, teachers were given opportunities to attend workshops that addressed developmentally appropriate curriculum and were provided with time to write minigrants that would fund new programs. To build home-school rapport and to bond strong relationships with parents, Currie added an element of fun (adult play) by having the school host bowling parties, picnics, ice cream socials, cookouts, and PTA dinners for families. He initiated parent-child gardening, lap-reading activities, and parent involvement in all aspects of planning for the new school.

As parents became partners in the educational setting, they participated with teachers as members of a primary experience committee that was challenged to develop alternative methods of instruction for kindergarten through second grade (Currie 1990). Parents were provided with child development workshops, received informational articles from Currie, and held open meetings to discuss their ideas and Currie's suggestions, such as moving away from letter grades and using a portfolio and developmental continuum approach to reporting to parents. Parents and teachers designed a K–2 program with cross-age groupings and with the same teacher assigned to a group for three years. The plan was approved by Currie and was put into operation.

Currie (personal communication, January 1, 1991) reports that the success of the pilot K–2 Primary Experience Program means that within two years there will be total school conversion. He describes what goes on during the school day as "guided learning," stating that he is a firm believer in play as a learning medium. All classrooms have learning centers and play materials for open-ended experiences where Currie observes five-, six-, and seven-year-olds spending time together at activities that some parents and teachers previously associated only with kindergarten. Currie spends a great deal of time "modeling the types of relationships that he wanted the faculty and children to develop" (1990, 33). *Once parents become partners, they will become advocates for developmentally appropriate curriculum at all levels of education.*

CONCLUSION

The creative teacher is the key to returning play to kindergarten and first grade classrooms. Creative teaching demands risk-taking and courageous behaviors from educators who have a strong background in early child development and education and who can articulate the value of their curriculum to administrators, colleagues, parents, and the general public.

Play's rightful place in the public school will be assured when teachers as child advocates begin to speak out on behalf of children. The five creative educators described here have taken the first steps for all of us.

REFERENCES

Babcock, H. L. 1986. Developing the Young Child's Language and Cognitive Experiences Through Sociodramatic Play. Doctoral practicum, Nova University, Fort Lauderdale, Fla.

Baroody, A. J. 1989. Manipulatives Don't Come with Guarantees. *Arithmetic Teacher* 37, no. 2: 4–5.

Bredekamp, S., ed. 1987. *Developmentally Appropriate Practice in Early Childhood Programs Serving Children from Birth Through Age 8.* Washington, D.C.: National Association for the Education of Young Children.

Currie, J. R. 1990. Unifying Faculty, Staff, Students, and Community by Establishing and Implementing a Unique Vision for a New Elementary School. Doctoral practicum, Nova University, Fort Lauderdale, Fla.

Dickerson, M. P. 1989. Designing an Instructional Program to Meet the Individual Needs of Kindergarten Children. Doctoral practicum, Nova University, Fort Lauderdale, Fla.

Doremus, V. P. 1986. Forcing Works for Flowers, but Not for Children. *Educational Leadership* 44, no. 3: 32–35.

Ellis, M. J. (1973). *Why People Play.* Englewood Cliffs, N.J.: Prentice Hall.

Freeman, E. B. 1990. Issues in Kindergarten Policy and Practice. *Young Children* 45, no. 4: 29–34.

Heimlich, J. E., and Pittelman, S. D. 1986. *Semantic Mapping: Classroom Applications.* Newark, Del.: International Reading Association.

Henniger, M. L. 1987. Learning Mathematics and Science Through Play. *Childhood Education* 63: 167–71.

Kubala, R. 1989. Improving the Receptive Vocabulary of Disadvantaged Kindergarten Students. Doctoral practicum, Nova University, Fort Lauderdale, Fla.

McCabe, J. S. 1978. *Characteristics of Classroom Environments and Their Relationships to Cognitive Development.* Report No. SPO12555. American Educational Research Association. ED 150 157.

Murphy, M. R. 1990. Enhancing Mathematics Problem-Solving Skills of 5- and 6-Year-Olds Through Explorative Learning Experiences. Doctoral practicum, Nova University, Fort Lauderdale, Fla.

Smilansky, S. 1968. *The Effects of Sociodramatic Play on Disadvantaged Preschool Children.* New York: Wiley.

Smilansky, S., and Shefatya, L. 1990. *Facilitating Play: A Medium for Promoting Cognitive, Socio-Emotional and Academic Development in Young Children.* Gaithersburg, Md.: Psychosocial and Educational Publications.

Sponseller, D. 1974. A Schema for Play and for Learning. In *Play as a Learning Medium*, edited by D. Sponseller, 115–23. Washington, D.C.: National Association for the Education of Young Children.

Stahl, S. A., and Vancil, S. J. 1986. Discussion Is What Makes Semantic Maps Work in Vocabulary Education. *Reading Teacher* 40: 62–67.

Zirbes, L. 1959. *Spurs to Creative Teaching.* New York: Putnam.

BIBLIOGRAPHY

Bemelmans, L. 1939. *Madeline.* New York: Viking.

Brown, M. 1947. *Stone Soup.* New York: Macmillan.

Leaf, M. 1989. *The Story of Ferdinand.* Cutchogue, N.Y.: Buccaneer Books. (Original work published 1941.)

Sendak, M. 1962. *Chicken Soup with Rice.* New York: Harper and Row.

Chapter 5

PLAY THEMES AND PROCESSES IN SEVEN- AND EIGHT-YEAR-OLDS

by Sara H. Arnaud

By the second and third grades most children have become sufficiently accustomed to school demands and expectations to have developed workable ways of navigating the system. On the whole, they are more comfortable and better organized than they were in the first grade. Many teachers report that second graders are far easier to teach than excitable, distractible first graders; seven- and eight-year-olds accept adult guidance with greater equanimity and can distinguish more readily between real and pretend.

These children have usually found suitable places in the school day to exercise their urges to play. The observing adult will readily see spontaneous play during recess, lunch time, and periods specifically set up for it by the teacher. Attentive observation will also reveal scraps and crumbs of play showing around the edges of many learning activities and most transitions (for instance, the quick karate feints of a boy getting up from his desk). At this age spontaneous play tends to become somewhat more formalized than it was previously. Even the earlier pell-mell of boy-girl run-and-chase becomes organized along gamelike lines, such as soccer and tag. Games with rules become increasingly important and are usually learned from older children or adults. The plots and actors in dramatic play call upon not only the child's own daily experience (e.g., playing school), but on the vicariously experienced figures of literature and television (e.g., enactment of violent scenes between the good and bad guys using GI Joe figures or Teenage Mutant Ninja Turtles).

Often there is a sort of interpenetration of game structure by elements of dramatic play. Such play may express, in symbolic ways, deep emotional concerns with which the child is struggling.

> *How intense worries and conflict may be expressed through game-playing is evident in a recess game a number of third-grade children I observed had developed and played avidly for weeks. It was called "Custody" and involved a child being summoned by one side or the other to the custody of Mother or Father, in a way analogous to Red Rover. The game was initiated by a boy whose parents were divorcing, an experience that was shared by several other children in the class and perhaps feared by still others. At any rate, the initiator's anguished uncertainty and feelings of helplessness were picked up and resonated to by enough other children to make this an exciting, if scary, game for them all.*

Peer interaction becomes all important for seven- and eight-year-olds. Friendships bloom and fade; enmities flourish and then abruptly end. Game demands for complexity of social group interaction vary. Children may play in pairs, as in cards, checkers, or dominoes; as individuals in small groups, as in marbles, skip rope, or Monopoly; or in teams, as in soccer, baseball, or hockey. Within the past decade, great numbers of children of this age spend hours in computer games alone or, most often, with a valued yet competitive friend. Team sports involving genuine intragroup cooperation and self-subordination are still extremely difficult for seven-year-olds. Though they may struggle mightily with the goal of team endeavor, it is very, very hard to sacrifice one's own star turn for the good of the team as a whole. They do much better with loosely organized team games, without specialized game roles, such as Red Rover. By age eight, some children do begin to manage cooperative team play, but they may find only one role on the team really appeals to them, the one with some individual emotional significance (such as the chronically angry little boy who finally settled implacably on the position of goalie).

In their intense awareness of other children and of status among peers, children of this age show great concern with who is "strongest," "smartest," "best." This is a time when management of anger, aggression, and fierce rivalry are urgent concerns for both girls and boys. One place these explosive impulses can be acceptably expressed is in games that are socially supported and approved—provided one follows the rules. After all, it is "just a game," not to be taken seriously, with no permanent consequences. If one loses this time, there's always another chance in the next game.

The child is beginning to learn to deal with the great, universal conflict between, on the one hand, the overweening wish to win with its glorious feeling of self-enhancement and the avoidance of the terrible feeling of defeat, and, on the other hand, the wish to keep oneself and one's opponent "honest." The hope of being a good sport is usually only a faint glimmer on the horizon.

A major developmental task of this age is the internalization of conscience and increasing moral self-regulation. Fairness and following the rules of the game become the rallying cry. "That's not fair!" and "Cheater! Cheater!" become playground anthems. At this age, rules are regarded as concrete, immutable, brooking no change or adjustment—that, at least, is the child's conscious ideal. So he or she constantly exhorts others not to cheat at games, to "follow the rules," while at the same time obstreperously denying any possibility that she herself has cheated, even when her breach has been plain for all to see.

At a symbolic level, many other common human concerns and problems are played out in the social setting of games, in a way that permits children to learn from each other. They see how others deal with such issues as exercising power or complying with others' power, dealing with "the luck of the draw," chance versus skill and competence, and how to conduct oneself in triumph and also in defeat. Children begin to safely develop and refine their own strategies for responding to such situations in ways that will help them maintain self-esteem while keeping other children's respect and liking.

Dramatic play is an enactment of fantasy, many elements of which may not be in the child's clear awareness—even for the child as cognitively advanced as the reading/writing eight-year-old. It may be primarily wish fulfilling, a dream of glory, or it may be a repetition of a gratifying experience. Or it may be used in an attempt to master a traumatic experience or other anxieties the child entertains. Sociodramatic play permits the child to deal with anxiety-provoking situations in acceptable, disguised, and moderate ways, often with a role reversal from victim to aggressor or power figure.

Dramatic play continues to be an important mode of expression for seven- and eight-year-olds, though it may tend to go underground and be hidden from adult eyes. Yet with a little encouragement and especially inviting space and materials (puppets, camcorder, or a stage area to present "the story"), children are quite willing, even eager, to play out their fantasies before adults if there is a matter-of-fact air of interest and approval.

Themes vary from placid to violent and gory. Domestic play with dolls persists (often with only mother and children, father not present). There are authoritarian enactments of demanding schoolteacher and recalcitrant pupils—here the action is usually initiated by the child who plays teacher. Sometimes the school scene is benevolent; at other times frightening possibilities may be featured—for example, the domineering, scolding, or punitive teacher or principal. Seven-year-olds may still need to play out the scary aspects of riding in the school bus. Through such play the child tries actively (albeit symbolically) to master what worries or frightens him.

A newly emerging theme is the parentless band of children (friends or siblings) who make their way together, often in wealth and power, and deal effectively with a sometimes dangerous world. Alternatively, the common foundling fantasy may be enacted in a scenario where children live gloriously with prestigious and powerful parents (kings and queens). By age eight, grisly plots begin to appear with supernatural figures and forces, death, and resurrection. In the plot, seemingly innocuous people may turn into dangerous criminals. All of this is usually accompanied by silliness and joking that serve to maintain the unreality of the story. It is helpful for the teacher to accept the silliness and self-consciousness natural to this age, but to set firm and clear limits to out-of-bounds behavior and wild excitability that can disrupt the play.

Encouraging children to express these common fantasies in writing stories and plays would be a further benefit, both educationally and emotionally. Remember that play, because it is spontaneous and highly enjoyable, functions as a natural energizer and organizer of cognitive learning in children.

Chapter 6

PLAY-FILLED LEARNING IN ONE SECOND GRADE

by Karen West

Play is a vital part in the learning process in our second grade classroom. I strive to create an environment of acceptance, creativity, communication, and openness. In this environment children make choices and use their own language in communicating with their classmates, which helps in solving their "real-world" problems. Children must feel that the classroom is their room and that they are each important players. Choices for children are essential. These choices may be as simple as choosing an activity for a book report or deciding how to measure a dinosaur. When this happens, children are more connected to the activity, they personalize their learning, and they are more likely to use their new-found skills again.

The teaching skills that I have found to be most helpful in connecting children's play with the structured curriculum in the public school setting are a keen sense of observation, communicating WITH children, and helping children connect thought with words. The ultimate goal is to help children give meaning to their world with others.

Examples of blending classroom subjects and play take many forms. Here are a few I have found effective.

Combining basic art skills with language activities produces interesting results. For example, using acorns, a cross section of an apple, paint, and a large sheet of paper, children can create from apple and acorn prints a meaningful background for practicing long and short vowel sounds.

Creative drama is a way for children to freely express themselves as individuals and to learn the basic art of cooperating in a group. They use their own language, organizational, and thinking skills. A science unit about weather came alive when the children listed winter activities and then acted them out. Laughter was heard throughout the pod as the children hit me with their imaginary snowballs. This activity involved logical and sequential thinking skills. You can't squeeze on your winter boots—even playfully in Florida!—without putting on your warm woolly socks first. You can't throw the snowball without first scooping and packing the snow.

Another important part of creative drama is giving other groups time to appreciate their performance. Parents, office staff, or anyone who would be an appreciative audience validates the children's reality, provides an opportunity for others to laugh at their humor, and builds self-confidence.

One item every clasroom must have is a "Prop Box." This is the source of a simple magical activity. In my classroom I have a large box. The children and I bring in anything no longer needed at home to add to the box and use it as a prop for creating characters and scenarios for skits. The children love dressing up to resemble their invented characters, ranging from mermaids to tourists. From scraps of material, hats, scarves, dishes, tools, and clothes, they create and perform.

Reading Huts, better known to some students as Reading Teepees, are long-remembered activities that connect children's play and reading. Children construct their reading huts from newspapers, tape, string, and sheets. A schematic drawing by one second grader showing how to construct a reading hut follows. In this activity children create a hut city in the classroom in which they can read by themselves or with a friend. Sometimes the teacher crawls in too.

Reading Tepies

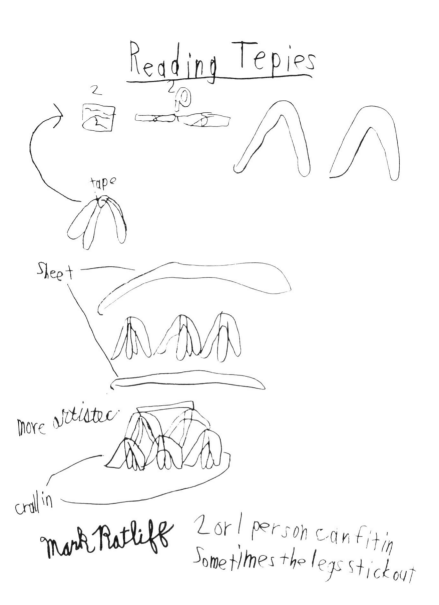

2

tape

Sheet

more artistec

crall in

Mark Ratliff

2 or 1 person can fit in
Sometimes the legs stick out

71

In summary, a teacher wishing to include play in the classroom setting must be a risk-taker, an expert in child watching, and someone who is able to connect children's thinking to meaningful activities that weave a tapestry between play and the structure of the school system.

Chapter 7

SOME THOUGHTS ABOUT PLAY

by Fred Rogers
with Hedda Bluestone Sharapan

THE IMPORTANCE OF PLAY

"Child's play" is one of the most misleading phrases in our language. We often use it to suggest something easy to do, something trivial, but it's not—not by any means. When children play, they're *working*. For them, play is both a serious and a necessary business, and it's one of the most important ways children learn and grow.

Because we deeply respect what play means to young children, we have always made play and pretend a significant part of whatever we present on "Mister Rogers' Neighborhood." On our "television visits" we talk about the things that matter in childhood, like feeling afraid at the emergency room, or worried about moving, or angry with a friend, and we generally go beyond talk . . . into *play*.

Some of that play can help children work out things going on in their own development. For example, if we're talking about how children feel when a parent goes away, I may play with a toy truck, making it go away somewhere but always come back, again and again. That kind of "child's play" can be very important in helping a child come to feel reassured that loved ones who have to leave for a while will come back.

We also encourage play that can help children rehearse events that may be difficult for them, like going to the hospital or leaving an old familiar home for a new one. When those concerns are part of our visits, I might use a toy stethoscope on a stuffed animal or pack up toy furniture to move to a new house made of blocks. With that kind of play, we can talk about what to expect, how we feel about that, and what we can do with those feelings.

At other times I may just be playful, running my fingers through the sand at our sandbox, or pouring water through a funnel at the sink, or making up silly rhyming sounds. Children's play can, of course, be just for the fun of it!

PRETENDING AND PLAY

Pretending is a particularly important part of play for young children. For example, when they're dressing up in grown-up clothes, children can pretend they are big and powerful and in charge of things for a change. Even little children need to *feel* in control of their world from time to time (without the scary responsibility of actually *being* in control), just as there are times of stress or uncertainty when they may need to feel smaller and younger than they really are. Then they can pretend to be a baby again.

A part of almost all our television visits takes place in the puppet kingdom that we call the Neighborhood of Make-Believe, a place for pretending. Our royal family—King Friday XIII, Queen Sara, and Prince Tuesday—lets us try out many feelings: how it might feel when a father gets angry, when parents have to go to work, or when it's time to start school. In one Make-Believe visit, Henrietta Pussycat thought her best friend didn't want to be her best friend anymore, and we practiced feelings about that. Through the puppet character, Lady Elaine Fairchilde, we have often played about how it feels to be a mischief maker who is unsure of the acceptance and approval of loved ones. What we try to do in these programs is to help children know that when the real people or real events in their lives make them puzzled or frightened, angry, or sad, pretending about those feelings (playing about them!) can be a safe way to work on them and keep them in control.

It's a way for them to grow on the inside, which is every bit as important as growing on the outside!

TELEVISION AND PLAY

I believe one of the best uses of television is as an encouragement for play. To help care givers use "Mister Rogers' Neighborhood" in that way, we developed our PLAN & PLAY book with a brief description of what's included in our program each day and suggestions for encouraging children to play about what they have seen. For a program in which we talk about bandages, in the PLAN & PLAY book we suggest that a teacher consider helping children make a pretend hospital for the dolls at the school. For a program about safety, in the book we describe ways of helping children make stop and go signs for their car play. As children play about the themes of a television program, *any* television program, they can have a more real and personal understanding of what they saw. This can be particularly important when children watch scary programs; their play afterwards can help them understand that what they saw was *not* real. There also may be times when the content of a program may be so upsetting that a child may not be able to put it into play and may need an adult's assurances that what he or she saw was not real.

We're always pleased to hear about children who have made their own playthings based on our program—trolleys from shoe boxes, or models of our Neighborhood of Make-Believe from clay or blocks. And we've been especially glad to know that our Neighborhood operas have inspired some wonderful creations from children, even very young ones. A three-year-old girl made up an "opera" about a pink monster in which she assigned the various roles to family members. Who got to play the central character of the pink monster? No one. That would have made the opera too scary. Several years ago a six-year-old sent us 11 pages of music paper with melodies and story about an owl and a tiger and an archaeologist. One of our most recent treasures was a videotape from a family who wrote and performed its own opera, "Won't You Be My Neighbor . . . or Won't You Have Some Fruitcake?" That opera was about new arrivals in the neighborhood who were unwanted by all except the young teddy bear next door. That teddy bear made overtures of friendship and fruitcake and finally influenced the others to welcome the newcomers. Of course most of the "reports" about children's creative use of our "Neighborhood" come through letters from parents and teachers. It's good to know that those children who are using our television offerings in such imaginative ways also have adults in their own personal lives who appreciate creativity and play.

ENCOURAGING PLAY

Encouraging children's creative play isn't only about helping to get it started; it also has to do with the caring ways we respond. One of our favorite stories about helpful ways adults can react to what children do in their play came to us through Dr. Margaret McFarland, our dear friend, mentor, and chief consultant for our television series for many years. Margaret had a remarkable gift of teaching through stories of real children and families, and since this book is dedicated to her, we thought it might be especially appropriate to tell you her story about a young girl we'll call "Dottie," who continually drew trees. As a kindergartner Dottie began a whole series of drawings and paintings of many different kinds of trees—colorful trees paired with barren trees that looked sad—and all her pictures contained one small and one large tree. Having followed Dottie's development through many play therapy sessions, Margaret strongly suspected that Dottie was using those two trees to express the natural feminine competitiveness she felt with her mother for her father's affections. She continued those paired-tree drawings for several years.

One day when Dottie was 12, she made a drawing that was dramatically different. She drew a single colorful tree, all by itself, and she drew it upside down. When asked about her drawing, Dottie said, "It's a girl, and she's talking on the telephone"—the first time she had ever suggested her trees were anything but trees. There might be many different ways to read a picture like that single tree coming at the end of that series of paired ones, but Margaret felt pretty sure that Dottie had begun to declare through her picture that she was an individual, that she had worked through her competitive feelings about her mom and dad, and that she could now take these feelings beyond the immediate family and into the outside world. There's something else that's important about Dottie's story. All through those years her family and her teachers had let her go on drawing trees in ways she wanted to, even in sad and angry ways when she felt like it. If she hadn't been allowed to draw what she felt, what do you suppose might have become of those feelings?

Stories like that from Margaret McFarland and from others have helped us understand in a very real way that children use their drawings, paintings, and sculptures, their toys and puppets, their dancing and their songs, to express what's inside of them. In fact, those are often the best ways children have to allow their feelings expression. It seems, then, that a helpful response begins with our respect for what children bring to their play and for what they get from it.

Children want the approval and love of the people they care most about; one way we can encourage creative play in our children is to show our approval of it. Often, quiet sincere interest can mean more to a child than extravagant praise. Asking a child what a picture is about, and then sitting down and really listening, conveys a lot more than a rave review, like "Boy, are you a great artist!" It's also easy for grown-ups to misunderstand children's artwork. Saying "That's really beautiful!" may not be what's called for when the splashes of reds and yellows and blacks are the expression of angry feelings. Some paintings aren't meant to be "beautiful." As most care givers know, just displaying a picture on a refrigerator or at the office can make a four-year-old as proud as an artist at a gallery opening.

We may never fully understand exactly what a child's creative efforts mean, but what's important is that we encourage children to discover their own uniqueness and help them develop its expression. That's one of the greatest gifts we can ever give.

Through our work on "Mister Rogers' Neighborhood," we are attempting in our way to provide a "safe" place for children's play, a place that's safe for whatever their feelings and needs may be. We hope that our television visits can support other care givers as they find their own ways to make safe play spaces for the children in their care. Knowing that what we do helps give "child's play" the importance it deserves makes all our efforts on television and off truly worthwhile.

RESOURCES

Mister Rogers' Plan & Play: Daily Activities from Mister Rogers' Neighborhood. Available from Family Communications, 4802 Fifth Avenue, Pittsburgh, PA 15213 ($14.95 plus $3.95 shipping and handling).

Mister Rogers' Playbook: Insights and Activities for Parents and Children, by Fred Rogers and Barry Head. Berkley Publishing Group. Available from Family Communications ($7.95 plus $3.00 shipping and handling).

For a catalog of all the resources available, write to:
Family Communications, Inc.
4802 Fifth Avenue
Pittsburgh, PA 15213

Part II

Curriculum and the Place of Play in Educating Young Children

Part II
INTRODUCTION

by Victoria Jean Dimidjian

The researchers and practitioners who described the value and central place of play in the young child's learning process in Part I share basic assumptions about early education and methods of teaching young children. Articulation of these commonalities helps to bridge Part I with Part II, where authorities from the same tradition explore concerns about play and curriculum. The common assumptions uniting authors in the two parts of this volume are

- Conviction that early education must be structured to be developmental, sequential, and progressive in philosophical approach, thus providing individualization to the current growth level of each child within the classroom, center, or program;
- Conviction that early education must be holistic and interactive in design, must develop the child's speaking, thinking, moving, and creating capacities in integrated curriculum experiences;
- Conviction that early childhood curriculum must be designed to affirm the ethnic, racial, and other social dimensions characteristic of children of a particular school and community, not children remade to fit a particular curriculum framework that may devalue or ignore such dimensions;
- Conviction that the classroom or child care environment should be designed to be a hands-on, experience-providing, activity-based learning area where children can act with increasing independence, initiative, and goal-directed behaviors;
- Conviction that the teacher-child relationship is a dynamic dyadic human relationship, is critical in the learning process, and is one to which each brings important ideas, experience, and input but in which teachers have significant power in

81

developing minds and personalities and responsibility for seeing that such development occurs;

- Conviction that all children have potential for fully competent functioning, no matter what disadvantages or barriers they may have experienced, and that developmentally attuned and committed teachers can assist their growth on a daily basis;
- Conviction that play and learning are inseparably linked in early years, and that children who are competent players are best prepared to become competent thinkers and doers in later schooling.

With these common convictions—based in research about developmentally appropriate early education and practice with children birth through eight years—the question then becomes one of translating such overarching beliefs into daily practices that occur in story time, in the creative arts area, during group music and movement activities, and in all the other parts of the lived curriculum as that curriculum unfolds each day between children and their teachers.

Part II of this volume seeks to assist in the translating process, examining pieces of the early childhood curriculum and exploring how play is best used as the vehicle of exploring, testing, and ultimately learning as the child actively uses the materials, guidance, and ideas that teachers make sure are provided daily. In Chapter 8, for example, Kamii and Lewis examine the efficacy of activity-based mathematics. At first glance this may appear as "just play with numbers," but it challenges the child's thinking and creative skills in addition to mastery of content. Similarly, Fennimore and Vold in Chapter 9 and Anderson and Fordham in Chapter 10 apply the same approach to multicultural and literacy education in the early years. Play, these authors agree, is at the heart of dynamic, interactive curriculum. In Chapter 11, Mendoza and Rubin follow this discussion by presenting a checklist process that can be used to critique the adequacy of the K–3 classroom's capacity to make play central in the learning process, as the previous chapters described. Use of this checklist can be valuable as a self-study tool for teachers trying to tranform their classrooms from one-way, didactic delivery structures into beehives of early learning, play-based buzz centers producing young independent achievers.

But what about the increasing numbers of children in early education who come to their first school experiences without the internal development that enables them to be competent players and speakers and drawers and doers in all the experiences just described? Wolfgang in Chapter 12 examines developmental issues inadequately resolved in the first years of life and proposes a paradigm of intervention for classrooms to help strengthen the ego development of three- to eight-year-olds. And in Chapter 13 therapist Carbonara and kindergarten teacher Scanlon summarize the careful and coordinated efforts that took place in the classroom, the home, and the treatment center, showing the increasing play skill and educational accomplishments of one nonplayer, first identifed by her nursery and family as needing help long before she began a cycle of failure to perform in "formal school."

Finally, chapters 14 and 15 address the broader implications of play's place in public education and in preparation of teachers for early childhood classrooms in the public schools. Schultz challenges his readers to "get serious" about play's power in home, community, and classroom settings. He voices concern about the detrimental effects that removal of the time, space, and affirmation of child's play may have on our nation's newest generation of learning little ones. Then Feeney examines issues in preparing early educators to have the understanding, skills, and commitment needed to create classrooms where play can thrive. Her call for revision of curriculum in teacher education, in certification of early educators, and in structure of systems of public education emphasizes the necessity of clearly defining the distinctiveness of early childhood education and of children's play taking a central place within that domain.

The underlying theme—valuing and affirming play's place in public education for young children—surfaces in all the chapters in Part II again and again as various concerns about early childhood curriculum are examined. Today we must be sure that play is central in the curriculum planning, delivery, and teacher preparation process. Young children who are communicative, cooperative players in their early years will most readily become the independent, thoughtful learners in their later years. Only by having teachers, schools, and educational systems that promote play as the young child's medium for learning will this be possible.

Chapter 8

PRIMARY ARITHMETIC: THE SUPERIORITY OF GAMES OVER WORKSHEETS

by Constance Kamii
and Barbara A. Lewis

Traditionally, the teaching of primary arithmetic has been based on the assumption that mathematics is a set of rules, facts, and symbols for the learner to internalize. However, the theory of Jean Piaget called "constructivism" has shown that young children acquire mathematical knowledge by constructing it from the inside, in interaction with the environment. The best way to explain this statement is by describing children's reactions to one of the tasks Piaget developed with Inhelder (Inhelder and Piaget 1963).

The child is given one of two identical glasses, and the teacher takes the other one. After putting 30 to 50 chips (or beans, buttons, etc.) on the table, the teacher asks the child to drop a chip into his or her glass each time she drops one into hers. When about five chips have thus been dropped into each glass with one-to-one correspondence, the teacher says, "Let's stop now, and you watch what I am going to do." The teacher then drops one chip into her glass and says to the child, "Let's get going again." The teacher and the child drop about five more chips into each glass with one-to-one correspondence, until the teacher says, "Let's stop." The following is what has happened so far:

Teacher: 1+1+1+1+1+1 +1+1+1+1+1
Child: 1+1+1+1+1   +1+1+1+1+1

The teacher then asks, "Do we have the same amount, or do *you* have more, or do *I* have more?"

Four-year-olds usually reply that the two glasses have the same amount. When we go on to ask, "How do you know that we have the same amount?" four-year-olds explain, "Because I can see that we both have the same amount." (Some four-year-olds reply, however, that *they* have more, and when asked how they know that they have more, their usual answer is "Because.")

The teacher goes on to ask, "Do you remember how we dropped the chips?" and four-year-olds usually give all the empirical facts correctly, including the fact that only the teacher put an additional chip into her glass at one point. In other words, four-year-olds remember all the empirical facts correctly yet base their judgment of equality on the empirical appearance of the two quantities.

By age five or six in kindergarten, however, most middle-class pupils deduce logically that the teacher has one more. When we ask these children how they know that the teacher has one more, they invoke exactly the same empirical facts as the four-year-olds.

No one teaches five- and six-year-olds to give correct answers to these questions. Yet children all over the world become able to give correct answers by constructing numerical relationships through their own natural ability to think. This *construction from within* can best be explained by reviewing the distinction Piaget made among three kinds of knowledge—physical knowledge, logico-mathematical knowledge, and social (conventional) knowledge—according to their sources.

Physical knowledge is knowledge of objects in external reality. The color and weight of a chip are examples of physical properties that are *in* objects in external reality and can be known empirically by observation.

Logico-mathematical knowledge, on the other hand, consists of *relationships* created by each individual. For instance, when we are presented with a red chip and a blue one and think that they are *different*, this difference is an example of logico-mathematical knowledge. The chips are observable, but the difference between them is not. The difference exists neither *in* the red chip nor *in*

86

the blue one, and if a person did not put the objects into this relationship, the difference would not exist for him or her. Other examples of relationships the individual can create between the chips are *similar, the same* in weight, and *two.*

Physical knowledge is thus empirical in nature because it has its source partly in objects. Logico-mathematical knowledge, however, is not empirical knowledge, as its source is in each individual's head.

The ultimate sources of *social knowledge* are conventions worked out by people. Examples of social knowledge are the fact that Christmas comes on December 25 and that a tree is called "tree." Words such as *one, two,* and *three,* and numerals such as 1, 2, and 3 belong to social knowledge, but the numerical concepts necessary to understand these numerals belong to logico-mathematical knowledge.

Keeping the distinction among the three kinds of knowledge in mind, one can understand why most four-year-olds in the task described earlier said that the two glasses have the same amount. The four-year-olds had not yet constructed the logico-mathematical relationship of number and could therefore gain only physical knowledge from the experience. From the appearance of the chips in the glasses, the children concluded that the amount was the same despite the fact that they remembered the way in which the chips had been dropped. Once the concept of number has developed, however, pupils will deduce from the same empirical facts that the teacher has one more chip regardless of the physical appearance.

NEW GOALS FOR PRIMARY ARITHMETIC

If children develop mathematical understanding through their own natural ability to think, the goals of primary arithmetic must be that children think, construct a network of numerical relationships, and invent their own procedures for solving problems. To add five and four, for example, children have to think $(1+1+1+1+1) + (1+1+1+1)$. This operation requires pupils to make two wholes (5 and 4) in their heads and then to make a higher-order whole (9) in which the original wholes (5 and 4) become parts. An example of a network of numerical relationships can be seen when pupils think about 5 + 4 as one more than 4 + 4, as one less than 5 + 5, as 5 + 2 + 2, etc.

This definition of goals for instruction is very different from traditional instruction that focuses on correct answers and the writing of mathematical symbols. It is also very different from the assumption that pupils have to internalize "facts" and rules, store them, and retrieve them in computer-like fashion.

According to constructivism, social interaction is essential for the development of logico-mathematical knowledge as well as for children's socio-moral development (Piaget 1932/1965, 1947/1963, 1948/1973). Piaget (1948/1973) stated that a classroom atmosphere that fosters conformity and submission in the socio-moral realm also fosters conformity and submission in the intellectual realm, and vice versa. Socio-moral development and intellectual development are thus inseparable for Piaget, and children's socio-moral development is an overarching goal for a constructivist teacher throughout the day.

GAMES

In this chapter, we will focus only on games and refer the reader to two books (Kamii 1985, 1989a) for the two other types of activities used in a constructivist primary mathematics program: the use of situations in daily living such as voting and discussions in groups to exchange ideas about different ways of solving problems (Kamii 1989b, 1990a, 1990b). Since many other games appropriate for grades one to three can be found in the two books, we will describe only five.

Tens

Two or three children can play this game, which uses 36 cards, four each of the numbers 1 through 9. One player makes a 3 x 3 arrangement with the top nine cards of the deck. The other cards are left face down in a stack near the playing area. The players take turns looking for all the pairs of cards that make a total of 10 (9 + 1, 8 + 2, etc.). When a player cannot find any more pairs, he fills in the empty places with cards from the pile, and the turn passes to the next person. The player who finds the most pairs is the winner.

Punta

Two to four people play this homemade card game. The deck consists of 60 cards, 10 each of the numbers 1 to 6. The game begins with all the cards dealt. One player then rolls two dice. Everybody tries to make the total of the two dice in as many ways as possible. For example, a total of 9 can be made with 6 + 2 + 1, 6 + 3, 5 + 4, 4 + 4 + 1, etc. The player who gets rid of all her cards first is the winner.

Multiples of 10

This game uses six 12-sided dice, and two to four people can play well together. The players take turns rolling all six dice and try to earn as many points as possible in multiples of 10. For example, if one player rolls 12, 9, 8, 5, 4, and 7, he may get only 20 points with 12 + 8. Someone else may have gotten 40 points with 12 + 8 + 7 + 4 + 9. The children keep score, and the player with the highest total at the end is the winner.

Salute!

Three players are needed for this game. All the cards 1 through 10 are dealt to two players, and each holds her stack face down. Simultaneously, the two players take the top cards of their respective piles and say "Salute!" as they hold the cards next to their faces in such a way that each can see only her opponent's card. The third player announces the sum of the two cards and says "Thirteen," for example. Each of the other two players deduces the number in her hand. The person who shouts the correct number first takes both cards. The winner is the person who collects the most cards.

Yahtzee

This game is well known and widely available in stores. Two to three players are ideal. The players take turns rolling five dice and recording their scores on a sheet that specifies how certain types of rolls should be scored (e.g., a player who has three of a kind counts the total number of points on the three dice). Some ways of accumulating points are more advantageous than others; the player with the most points at the end is the winner.

Advantages of Games
over Worksheets

The following five advantages of games can be compared with the disadvantages of worksheets:

1. *In games the motivation to work comes from children.* Children beg to play games. In contrast, most children complete worksheets because they are externally motivated by grades or stickers or afraid of consequences such as missing recess. Young children do not have to be bribed or threatened to learn. When children learn for their own reasons (the pleasure of playing with other children and the challenge to master the tasks of the particular game), their initiative and cognitive abilities develop from within.

2. *In games children invent their own strategies and ways of achieving their goals.* If children can play a board game with one die, for example, we simply introduce a second die and let them figure out what to do. By contrast, traditional mathematics instruction shows children how to add single- and multidigit numbers. In playing Punta, to cite another example, some first graders start with small numbers, quickly use up their 1s and 2s, and get stuck with five and six cards. Others try to use up their 6s

and 5s first. When worksheets are used, children repeat the same kind of calculation over and over, with only slight variations in the numbers. Worksheets thus promote mechanical repetition and mental passivity.

3. *In games children supervise and correct each other.* If one player takes a 3 and an 8 in Tens, for example, another player is likely to object immediately. Immediate feedback from a peer is much more effective than worksheets corrected by the teacher. Worksheets are usually returned the next day, and young children cannot remember and do not care about what they did yesterday. They are thus ready to make the same errors day after day. Furthermore, through worksheets, children learn that only the teacher can tell whether or not an answer is correct. This learned dependency on adults is the opposite of becoming confident in one's own ability to figure things out.

4. *In games children have the opportunity to develop socially and morally.* Conflicts are bound to arise in games, and children have the possibility of deciding who goes first, what to do with a player who does not follow the rules, etc. Children also have the responsibility of deciding how many rounds will constitute a game if a game seems too short. Worksheets make children work alone, thereby depriving them of opportunities to develop socially or morally. We hear a great deal about the need for drug education and for sex education to prevent AIDS and teenage pregnancy. These problems are caused less by children's ignorance about drugs, AIDS, and pregnancy, however, than by their inability to make independent judgments, resisting peer pressure. We urgently need to strengthen children's social and moral development throughout the day.

5. *In games, the teacher can assess children's processes of thinking because the same game is usually played at different levels.* In playing Tens, for example, some children count the symbols on the cards by trial and error. Others look for a 3 if they find out that 7 + 4 = 11. Some know 5 + 5 and 9 + 1 but not the other combinations. At the end of this game, some children know that they can take all the remaining cards, while others cannot find any pair even after counting the symbols by trial and error! By

contrast, when the teacher corrects worksheets, she cannot know *how* a child got an answer.

Although games offer many advantages, these are not automatically realized. We therefore conclude with two frequently found errors to avoid when instituting activity-based arithmetic games.

Two Errors to Avoid

First, the teacher must play games with children instead of using this time to correct papers. If the teacher is not directly engaged, children quickly get the message that games are not important enough for the teacher to bother with. When the teacher sits down to play with children, however, this encourages them to think harder at higher levels, and enables the teacher to get the best diagnostic information.

Second, the teacher needs to work on children's development of autonomy (i.e., becoming able to govern oneself) instead of expecting games to go independently and smoothly from the beginning. It is natural for children to come to the teacher with complaints such as "So-and-so won't let me have a turn." The teacher needs to refrain from solving these problems for children and, instead, to tactfully suggest ways for children to solve their own problems, assisting them directly only if an impasse occurs.

The need for reform of mathematics education is too well known to repeat here (National Council of Teachers of Mathematics 1989; National Research Council 1989). In primary arithmetic, the reform of the 1980s used achievement tests and worksheets, which aggravated the problems of mental passivity, dependence on adult authority, blind conformity, and submissiveness. We hope the reform of the 1990s will focus more on children's critical thinking, autonomy, creativity, and initiative in mathematics as well as in the socio-moral realm.

REFERENCES

Inhelder, B., and Piaget, J. 1963. De l'Itération des Actions à la Récurrence Élémentaire. In *La Formation des Raisonnements Récurrentiel,* edited by P. Greco, B. Inhelder, B. Matalon, and J. Piaget, 151–227. Paris: Presses Universitaires de France.

Kamii, C. 1985. *Young Children Reinvent Arithmetic.* New York: Teachers College Press.

_____. 1989a. *Young Children Continue to Reinvent Arithmetic, Second Grade.* New York: Teachers College Press.

_____. 1989b. *Double-Column Addition: A Teacher Uses Piaget's Theory.* Videotape. New York: Teachers College Press.

_____. 1990a. *Multiplication of Two-Digit Numbers: Two Teachers Using Piaget's Theory.* Videotape. New York: Teachers College Press.

_____. 1990b. *Multidigit Division: Two Teachers Using Piaget's Theory.* Videotape. New York: Teachers College Press.

National Council of Teachers of Mathematics. 1989. *Curriculum and Evaluation Standards for School Mathematics.* Reston, Va.: NCTM.

National Research Council. 1989. *Everybody Counts: A Report to the Nation on the Future of Mathematics Education.* Washington, D.C.: National Academy Press.

Piaget, J. 1963. *The Psychology of Intelligence.* Paterson, N.J.: Littlefield, Adams. (Original work published 1947)

_____. 1965. *The Moral Judgment of the Child.* New York: Free Press. (Original work published 1932)

_____. 1973. *To Understand Is to Invent.* New York: Grossman. (Original work published 1948)

Chapter 9

EDUCATION TODAY FOR A MULTICULTURAL WORLD

by Beatrice S. Fennimore
and Edwina B. Vold

The complete education gives one not only the power of concentration but worthy objectives upon which to concentrate. The broad education will, therefore, transmit to one not only the accumulated knowledge of the race but all the accumulated experience of social living.

—Martin Luther King

Every realistic classroom teacher of young children will acknowledge the differences in characteristics, personal experiences, and interests among his or her students. It is the talented teacher who can meet those differences with enthusiasm and creativity. Current focus on multicultural education merely expands on the understanding and acceptance of anticipated differences among individuals in any given group. The expansion, which is relevant—even critical—for every classroom teacher, focuses on the gender, age, ability, and racial and cultural dimensions of each student's identity (Boyer 1985) in the classroom, the community, and society as a whole. Meaningful multicultural experiences belong in every early childhood classroom in rural, suburban, and urban communities—whether the classroom population is homogeneous or heterogeneous in nature. The heart and soul of multicultural education is visible, affirming respect for each individual in the classroom and equal respect for all others in the world.

Americans are a multicultural nation made up of people from different religions, ethnic backgrounds, native languages, and socioeconomic levels (Gollnick and Chinn 1983). Too many young children in classrooms, however, have experienced only a monocultural perspective, excluding the values, customs, history, and access to power of "minorities"—especially people of color (Ramsey, Vold, and Williams 1989). The current movement toward true multicultural educational approaches requires a comprehensive shift in attitudes and behaviors among teachers whose training may have been devoid of necessary information on the positive treatment of student diversity. This chapter can assist all teachers in *facing* the reality of widespread and increasing diversity in students' family, cultural, and socioeconomic lives; in *focusing* on a positive multicultural attitude that is based on high expectations, commitment to equity, and advocacy for children; and in *forming* a classroom approach that integrates appropriate play and activities with relevant multicultural experiences for all children.

FACING THE REALITIES OF DIVERSITIES

Racial, cultural, and socioeconomic diversities have long been a part of American history. These diversities, however, have either been ignored or assumed to eventually "melt" into a common American identity. Only now are many classroom teachers being called upon to recognize and value diversities and to respond to all children in a positive, equitable manner. These teachers are being asked to recognize the fact that our society has actively resisted acceptance of some minority children and their families. They are also now being required to recognize that the unparalleled economic boom following World War II, which enabled one parent (usually the father) to support the family while the other parent (usually the mother) tended to home and children, has declined (Rosewater 1989). Many teachers are now faced with this statistical reality: one in five American children is living in poverty, one in six has no health insurance, one in seven is at risk of dropping out of school, and one of two children has a mother in the work force in a society with very limited options for quality child care (Edelman 1989). The effective teacher cannot focus on what has been perceived as the conventional "ideal" since these "ideal" conditions are no longer possible for a majority of American families.

These facts form a complex maze for teachers who may already feel underpaid, overworked, and discouraged about conditions in their classrooms and in society. How can teachers in classrooms filled with young children form and support a multicultural environment within the context of social realities and professional expectations? The answer to that question is important—because children cannot experience a multicultural classroom until teachers have formulated positive multicultural attitudes and true personal appreciation of diversity.

FOCUSING ON POSITIVE MULTICULTURAL ATTITUDES

Almost all classroom teachers were once young college students who chose the field of education because they really believed they could make a difference. That belief does not have to change or disappear. Yes, society has changed for children and for adults—but the need is even greater for positive, productive, reflective teachers of young children. There was never a more important time for teachers to focus on building and maintaining a positive multicultural attitude. *Every child* needs to function successfully in a multicultural world, so every child needs and deserves to be prepared to accept diversity in a positive and productive way.

Three critical educational areas can contribute to the formation of a multicultural attitude:

1. Dedication to an equitable opportunity for all children to be exposed to excellence in education, enabling them to reach their highest potential (Smith 1989)
2. Awareness of the importance of high teacher expectations for all children because expectation definitely affects student outcomes

97

3. Advocacy, or the commitment of all teachers to active involvement in the lives of children beyond paid remuneration with the goal of enhancing opportunities for optimal personal growth and development (Fennimore 1989).

All too often, visitors to public school classrooms hear children discussed in negative tones. As a result, a classroom of lively and promising individuals can become stratified. "This type of child" from "that kind of community" or "that sort of family" can attract unfairly lowered expectations and inappropriately altered curriculum. Multicultural education demands that teachers accept and value diversity even when it means that children come from single-parent families, or foster care, or from a community where the majority of families require public assistance. The teacher with a multicultural attitude has a vision of human potential and a desire to build self-esteem and respect for others into the classroom approach for every single child.

To build and sustain a multicultural attitude, teachers need the overriding philosophy that respects cultural and individual differences of all people regardless of their racial, ethnic, cultural, or religious differences, backgrounds, or physical differences (Grant 1977). Most American teachers have been exposed to prejudice in their own backgrounds. Therefore it is not the denial of prejudice but the stated intent to recognize and rise above it that enriches and protects the multicultural attitudes of teachers.

FORMING A PLAY-BASED MULTICULTURAL CLASSROOM APPROACH

The goals of multicultural classroom approaches are to help children develop positive identities and develop their ability to identify, empathize with, and relate to individuals from other groups. This requires development of respect, concern for, and interest in others (Ramsey 1987). It is up to teachers to develop play activities that foster these goals; teachers must therefore recognize the issues in their communities and schools that might either undermine or encourage the multicultural approach.

Because classrooms do not exist in vacuums, teachers as curriculum planners and advocates must reflect on the messages in overall school policies for young children (Fennimore 1989). Does an in-school attitude exist that some children have less potential because they are less advantaged than children in other schools? Fairness demands that all children be discussed and taught in a respectful and encouraging manner. Is there any kind of tracking or labeling that creates an impression that some children are more "deserving" of excellent curriculum than others? The multicultural teacher must be resolved to treat every child equitably regardless of labels.

Is there a policy assumption that the "less advantaged child" does not have "time to play in school"? Teachers must be prepared to articulate and defend the multicultural belief that diversity in race, cultural, or socioeconomic status need not and should not dictate differentiated curriculum opportunities. Developmentally appropriate curriculum is based on knowledge of child development that spans complex differences in human characteristics and experiences. Some educators are convinced that teacher-directed instruction with academic objectives is necessary for at-risk children. They point to higher standardized scores as a positive result of direct instruction (Gerston and Keating 1987). Other educators focus on commonalities in early childhood curriculum, emphasizing child-initiated activity for all young students because it fosters respect for developmental limits and opportunities for differing potentials, and it encourages reciprocal and open-ended communication (Schweinhart 1988). Multicultural play-based activities do more than furbish young minds for immediate results in test scores—they form them for long-term results in the development of cognitive structures (DeVries and Kohlberg 1987).

Young children view their physical worlds and integrate information through lenses that reflect their racial, cultural, class, and individual experiences (Ramsey 1987). Effective classroom teachers therefore confirm the ways in which individual children think and learn; at the same time they affirm the diversity in the way individuals think and learn. These teachers have can-do classrooms with can-do activities and can-do children (Wasserman 1990). Workbooks or dittos are only a small or even nonexistent part of a classroom world of activities that challenge the capabilities of all students in relevant, realistic ways. The success and self-esteem of children at any achievement level is the ladder to more success and enhanced self-confidence.

What about required curriculum? What about the tests that have some amount of teacher accountability for results? The multicultural teacher of young children in public schools meets the requirements of employment in an ethical and professional way. That same teacher enhances curriculum through mediating, supplementing, enhancing, and interpreting approaches to social studies, language arts, science, mathematics, and all other curriculum areas. *What* is taught may be established in requirements, but *the way* it is taught is directly up to the teacher.

What can the teacher of young children do to form a multicultural classroom? Take a good look at the curriculum and decide on ways to enhance and supplement it with art, artifacts, library books, and a multitude of active hands-on experiences for children. These materials should reflect the lives, families, communities, interests, and learning styles of the children in the classroom. Photographs of families, homes, and community should be present; these should include photographic representations of the children themselves. (If your school cannot afford a camera, perhaps one can be donated.) Since the preoperational child is constructing physical knowledge in a social context through perceptions, relationships, environment, and spatial, temporal, and quantitative relationships (Ramsey 1987), manipulation of material and interactive discussion should take place in cooperative learning opportunities.

Simple materials such as food or clothing can be studied to observe similarities and differences. (Ethnic breads or different forms of pasta are very effective for such activities.) Teachers should develop a comfort level in pointing out and discussing differences in housing, families, and experiences. Differences in skin color should be discussed as openly as differences in eye or hair color. Young children are aware of problems asociated with a lack of fairness; they can even become "multicultural activists" in solving problems in the classroom. (How can John join in when he is in a wheelchair? Let's think of a way to welcome our new friend who does not understand our language yet.) (Derman-Sparks 1989). Like the young children in their classrooms, teachers can continually study, explore, and reflect on ways that promote multicultural learning in developmentally appropriate ways.

A good start for preoperational children—one that enables them to develop skills for continuing thinking, exploring, and learning—will lead naturally into further cognitive growth as children become concrete learners in the later early childhood years. For the child entering concrete operations, reversible and internalized actions will help to organize multicultural activities. No longer perceptually bound, young children from six to eight years of age will be even more receptive to concrete activities with real objects, things, and people that simultaneously increase their esteem for themselves and others. An excellent example would be a young child who enters school with a primary language other than English. When initial play-based learning experiences serve to affirm culture and language, the child will have the skills and confidence to explore other ways of acting and speaking during the concrete operational years.

SUMMARY

This chapter begins and ends with an affirmation of the fact that teachers make all the difference in the success or failure of multicultural education for young children. Since children will not believe what teachers themselves do not believe and put into practice, the important first step is for teachers to face the realities of children in America and then form an accepting and enhancing multicultural philosophy and curriculum-in-action. Teachers and children together in public schools can continually learn self-respect and respect for all others through meaningful, active, relevant multicultural classroom activities.

REFERENCES

Boyer, J. B. 1985. *Multicultural Education: Product or Process?* Kansas City: Kansas Urban Education Center.

Derman-Sparks, L., and the A.B.C. Task Force. 1989. *Anti-Bias Curriculum: Tools for Empowering Young Children.* Washington, D.C.: National Association for the Education of Young Children.

DeVries, R., and Kohlberg, L. 1987. *Constructivist Early Education: Overview and Comparison with Other Programs.* Washington, D.C.: National Association for the Education of Young Children.

Edelman, M. W. 1989. Children At Risk. In *Caring for America's Children,* edited by F. J. Macchiarola and A. Gartner, 20–30. New York: Academy of Political Science.

Fennimore, B. S. 1989. *Child Advocacy for Early Childhood Educators.* New York: Teachers College Press.

Gerston, R., and Keating, T. March 1987. Long-Term Benefits from Direct Instruction. *Educational Leadership* 44: 28–31.

Gollnick, D. M., and Chinn, P. C. 1990. *Multicultural Education in a Pluralistic Society.* 3d ed. Columbus, Ohio: Merrill.

Grant, G., ed. 1977. *In Praise of Diversity: Multicultural Classroom Applications.* Omaha: University of Nebraska at Omaha.

King, M. L. 1987. *The Words of Martin Luther King, Jr.* New York: Newmarket Press.

Ramsey, P. G. 1987. *Teaching and Learning in a Diverse World: Multicultural Education for Young Children.* New York: Teachers College Press.

Ramsey, P. G.; Vold, E. B.; and Williams, L. R. 1989. *Multicultural Education: A Source Book.* New York: Garland Publishing.

Rosewater, A. 1989. Child and Family Trends: Beyond the Numbers. In *Caring for America's Children,* edited by F. J. Macchiarola and A. Gartner, 4–19. New York: Academy of Political Science.

Schweinhart, L. J. May 1988. How Important Is Child-Initiated Activity? *Principal:* 6–10.

Smith, M. M. 1989. Excellence and Equity for America's Children. In *Early Childhood Education 90/91,* edited by J. S. McGee and K. M. Pacoriek, 12–17. Guilford, Conn.: Dushkin Publishing.

Wasserman, S. 1990. *Serious Players in the Primary Classroom.* New York: Teachers College Press.

Chapter 10

PLAY, RISK-TAKING, AND THE EMERGENCE OF LITERACY

by Ann E. Fordham
and William W. Anderson

Perhaps in no other area of human concern is the paradoxical relationship between risk-taking and being at risk so apparent as it is in language/literacy development. Research about literacy processes makes it clear that risk-taking is a fundamental prerequisite for fluent reading. Children who are afraid to risk rarely become fluent readers. They shrink from the venturesome activity that is essential for literacy to flourish. Forced attention to an intricate set of unreliable and confusing rules takes precedence over natural tendencies to explore with language, to play and experiment with print.

Why are risk-taking and reading ability so tightly intertwined? Reasons for this symbiotic relationship become clear upon review of insights accumulated through research in language/literacy development processes over the past ten years.

It is axiomatic among reading researchers that risk-taking occupies a central role in the literacy development process. The news media regularly exaggerate differences of opinion among literacy development researchers and suggest erroneously that such differences are somehow more pronounced and acrimonious than is true in other areas of scholarly pursuit. The reality is, however, that a broad consensus exists about the fundamental ingredients of a supportive environment for literacy growth. This is not to ignore the many healthy disagreements and lively debates among literacy researchers as to the precise nature of the process. It is striking to note, however, that—despite public perception to the contrary—there is a substantial degree of consensus on major issues. This high level of consensus is particularly apparent with respect to recognizing the role of risk-taking as a critical factor in literacy learning.

Most recent textbooks in reading pedagogy and basal reader programs acknowledge the importance of risk and guide teachers in the development of strategies for encouraging children to predict outcomes and explore possibilities in literature. Declining scores on the National Assessment of Educational Progress (NAEP) in thinking skills highlight the consequences of failure to encourage risk-taking behaviors involved in independent thinking and critical reflection. This has led to a widespread concern about students' difficulty with problem solving and critical thinking. Notwithstanding the evidence, many have difficulty in acknowledging that which seems obvious to those who have studied the needs of young children: *play is a key factor that cements the fundamental connection between risk-taking behavior and literacy growth.*

LITERACY DEVELOPMENT PROCESSES: IMPLICATIONS FOR PLAY

A review of current understandings of what it means to be literate, what capable readers and writers do, and how such competence develops provides insights about the important role of play in this process.

Under the influence of behaviorism, reading was for many years thought to be a simple linear process based upon the accumulation of hierarchical skills. The key to success was seen as systematic instruction, drill, and practice. Meaning-making, problem solving, and social interaction were viewed as unimportant and play was often considered to be a distraction from time on task and from the critical business of skill mastery. Its value was seen almost exclusively as a reinforcer to reward the "real" work of reading.

Further, the hierarchy that seemed logical to basic skills proponents placed reading as a prerequisite for writing.

Proponents of such a "bottom-up," parts-to-whole view of literacy have never been able to demonstrate that such a skill hierarchy actually exists. Rather, "reading" appears to be most aptly described as a holistic, interactive process of meaning-making and pattern recognition.

Also, it has become clear from emergent literacy research of the last decade (Teale and Sulzby 1986; Strickland and Morrow 1989a and 1989b; Ferreiro and Teberosky 1982) that writing development parallels or even precedes reading. There is growing consensus that skill-focused, bottom-up views of the process are dated and grossly inaccurate. This is reflected in the research synthesis *Becoming a Nation of Readers* (Anderson et al. 1985).

The emergent literacy process according to Ferreiro and Teberosky (1982) is one that largely transcends differences in language and culture. Such differences seem much more consequential between home and school environments than they are across linguistic and cultural groups (Wells 1986). To the extent, however, that a child's culture may diminish the value of play and impose unacceptable costs for risk-taking, literacy development cannot flourish.

In summary, reading is best understood as a complex process that includes such play-related components as risk-taking, negotiating of roles, problem solving, giving meaning to experience, active questioning, purposeful involvement, symbolic representation, social interaction, decontextualizing of experience, and awareness of sociolinguistic subtleties. It is little wonder that Albert Einstein referred to reading as the most complex task that humans must undertake.

The "why" of play is quite clear from even this cursory review of research in literacy processes. Specifically what, however, does play contribute to one's becoming literate? How can concerned adults support the play of children in ways that optimize literacy development? What are the issues in schools and society that impinge upon children's right to be children and to actualize their need to play? And finally, what do these questions imply for an action plan to improve the circumstances for children regarding their play and literacy development?

BECOMING LITERATE: THE ROLE OF PLAY

On the surface, one might wonder about the role of play in becoming literate. The term "literacy" evokes images of sedentary interactions with books, paper, and pencils. "Play," on the other hand, elicits images of spontaneous encounters with a variety of materials from sand and water to blocks and teddy bears. How, indeed, are the two related? The relationship of becoming literate and play becomes apparent as we look beyond the surface appearance to the underlying meanings that children derive from play and make use of in becoming literate. Specifically, play brings understanding of such literacy-related concepts as symbols, decontextualized language, the role of readers/writers, and the usefulness of print.

The use of symbols, the substitution of one thing in place of another, is a readily apparent characteristic of language. For example, a child comes to realize that the word "mama" stands for the person. The printed version "mama" is perhaps the most sophisticated example of symbolic representation. Making the transition in understanding between knowing "mama," the person, to saying the name and then to reading and writing the name comes gradually over time. Playful interactions with objects are instrumental in a child's understanding of symbols. "This Little Piggy Went to Market" recited in conjunction with touching each toe, is a familiar example of using symbols with young children. The smiles relate to the understanding that toes stand for piggies. Similarly, five raised fingers represent five little monkeys in a finger play. So too blocks become symbols for roads, towers, and houses, in the same manner that paint and crayons on paper are used to represent flowers, cats, or dogs. Or the kitchen broom may be transformed into a trotting pony for a child to straddle and ride across the living room. Thus, children grow in understanding of symbolic representation as they manipulate familiar objects and assign meanings to them. Children who are steeped in these playful pastimes are well equipped to assign meaning to the symbols of printed language.

Children who are becoming literate learn that book language sounds different from everyday talk in that the writer has to fill us in on so many things that are taken for granted in our common conversation. For example, in conversation, we make use of facial and body gestures to get our message across. We are often in the midst of the very things we are talking about, so there is little need to tell about them. Or, when we sit down for dinner and see steam rising from a bowl of chicken soup, simply saying "It's hot!" is enough to get our message across. That is rarely so for book language. The room, the people, and the bowl will most likely be described. The elaborated language of books is referred to as "decontextualized language" because of its distinctiveness from conversation (contextualized language that denotes its presence or context in the midst of objects and events that are being discussed). Being read to and hearing book language regularly is an excellent way to become familiar with decontextualized language. Another important way to gain this sense of language difference is for children to engage in dramatic play.

When children engage in dramatic play with others, they use decontextualized language to describe make-believe roles and situations. For example, one child may say, "You are the baby, and I am the mommy. This can be your stroller, and this can be my purse. Let's play like we're going to the mall." They are defining the context for their play. *In so doing, they are moving away from the concrete language of everyday conversation and moving toward the abstract language found in books, requiring an elaboration of setting, characters, and events.* Children who participate in dramatic play with others are bridging into the decontextualized language of books (Pellegrini 1985).

One characteristic of children involved in dramatic play is that they often spend more time talking about the way the role will be played out than they do in the actual role. For example, children will spend time negotiating how the baby is to fulfill the role—sleeping, waking, taking a bottle, crying, conversing with mama, or trying to climb out of the stroller. And mama, will she be looking for her shopping list, waving to a friend, admonishing the baby to stay seated in the stroller, standing in the checkout line, or trying on a new coat? The negotiation between the children about the nature of the roles each will play gives them a sense of different types of characters' expected behaviors and a basis for rational prediction when these roles are encountered in stories and books. Also, the give-and-take between the children concerning their separate roles requires a venture into a context removed from the present. Language shifts from here-and-now contextualized conversation to a make-believe "then-and-there" decontextualized conversation.

A language shift comes about naturally in children's dramatic play and serves as a bridge to the language of books. Thus, dramatic play provides opportunities for children to recall and reenact experiences, explore different roles, and construct contexts through props and language. The low-risk nature of dramatic play (i.e., the focus on process versus established outcomes as well as involvement with familiar scenarios and props) enables children to take risks in their explorations of roles and accompanying language.

One of the best ways to immerse children in language that is uniquely meaningful and relevant to their experiences is in the context of play. Increasingly, researchers and teachers are making the most of the connection between language learning and its utility by purposefully arranging settings for dramatic play that promote literacy-related behaviors (Schickedanz 1986; Strickland and Morrow 1989a, 1989b; Neuman and Roskos 1990). Props are added to traditional play areas and special themed play settings are created to facilitate these responses. For example, in the familiar house area, the teacher adds a phone book, calendar, note pad, and pencil to accompany the telephone. A cookbook, grocery coupons, recipe box, index cards, and pencil are additions to other necessities in the kitchen and dining area.

Themed settings for play also promote literacy-related behaviors. Teachers can extend children's play from the traditional house area by creating an adjoining dramatic play area such as a grocery store, restaurant, post office, or doctor's office. In these settings, children can engage in dramatic play that includes literacy-related behaviors in natural and useful ways. For example, the setting of a well-known local fast-food restaurant can be created and marked with a posted sign and the "special" for the day. Menus with bright pictures and accompanying print can be placed at a small table with chairs. Children can take roles as customers or servers and peruse the menu or write down orders on special pads of paper. Picturing this enticing play scenario, it is not surprising that "one study indicates that the amount of literacy activity in play increases significantly when teachers add reading and writing materials based on a specific theme in a play area as opposed to the usual dramatic play materials, such as blocks, kitchen items, dress-ups" (Strickland and Morrow 1989a, 178).

Humor is another form of play that naturally engages young children and may be successfully linked to literacy activities. Schickedanz, Hansen, and Forsythe (1990) trace the developmental progression of children's response to humor with implications for literacy assessment. For example, absurdities have great appeal to preschoolers who delight in recognizing incongruities as evidence of their understanding of the world. "Hey, Diddle, Diddle, the Cat and the Fiddle" from Mother Goose, and P. D. Eastman's *Are You My Mother?* (1960) are examples of this type of humor. Many first graders respond to humor based on phonological or sound ambiguity (e.g., "Knock, knock" jokes such as: "Who's there?" "Dwayne." "Dwayne who?" "Dwayne the tub; I'm dwowning."). The appeal of manipulating language in ways previously impossible is evident in their enjoyment of music, such as Raffi songs (e.g., "Willoughby, wallaby we; an elephant sat on me . . ." or "I like to eat, eat, eat, apples and bananas; I like to oat, oat, oat, oaples and banonos . . ."). By second grade, most children take pleasure in humor based upon lexical ambiguity, such as jokes with multiple meanings of words (e.g., "Why did the farmer name his hog Ink?" "Because he kept running out of the pen?"). Similar language play based on multiple meanings of words is found in the popular Amelia Bedelia series by Peggy Parish and the poetry of Jack Prelutsky.

Linking these engaging, listening/singing experiences with printed counterparts becomes a powerful vehicle for children's literacy. Teachers can print well-known songs and poems on large charts and track the words with a pointer as children watch and read chorally. Children can illustrate individual copies and keep them in special poetry folders or booklets to be read and enjoyed at school and at home.

RECOMMENDATIONS

If parents, care givers, and teachers are to promote literacy development in ways that truly serve children's needs, they must affirm the important role of play and systematically support it as an essential ingredient of development. To provide for better support of literacy-related play, some clear courses of action seem to us to be in order. These include:

- Creation of "risk-taking safety nets" through a climate that encourages exploration and questioning, one that values good questions more than "right" answers
- Avoidance of competitive games that place a premium on right answers or skilled performance as a measure of how well one did. Rather, select games and activities that build a sense of mutual support and that reward engagement in the process.
- Reexamination of the issue of control in literacy development and encouragement of learning environments in which children have regular opportunities to exercise many options while using language as a tool for exploration
- Promotion of the development of guidelines by professional organizations for minimal play time and

appropriate play environments in child care agencies and in schools

- Inclusion of play-related issues and ways to support literacy-related play as an important part of the curriculum in preparation programs for teachers and child care providers
- Reexamination of programs for at-risk children, such as Chapter I, and removal of highly structured controls that ignore the value of play and play-related activities.

CONCLUSION

This chapter has raised eight major issues examining play and literacy in young children. Any one of these issues could well become the topic of a book. Hence, we do not presume to do more than to heighten readers' awareness of the vital relationship between literacy development and play, to raise some issues not considered before, and to suggest some sources for further study.

Failure to value and support play will at best complicate the task of becoming literate and limit its pleasures. At worst, it may lead to illiteracy and adults ill equipped to deal with the world. Efforts to speed the pace of learning at the expense of play are tragic and costly. These costs are seen in limited literacy development with its inevitable economic consequences and in the need for myriad remedial measures.

As Camus noted in *The Plague* (1948), "The evil that is in the world always comes of ignorance, and good intentions may do as much harm as malevolence, if they lack understanding." Constructive change will occur and children's lives will be enriched only as progress is made in helping teachers, care givers, parents, and policymakers to understand the central role of play in becoming literate. Those armed with such understanding can then become powerful advocates for children's rights to be children and guarantee for them the opportunity to enjoy the play experiences that they so badly need for literacy and for life.

REFERENCES

Anderson, R. C., et al. 1985. *Becoming a Nation of Readers: The Report of the Commission on Reading.* Washington, D.C.: U.S. Government Printing Office.

Camus, A. 1948. *The Plague.* New York: Modern Library.

Eastman, P. D. 1960. *Are You My Mother?* New York: Beginner Books, Random House.

Ferreiro, E., and Teberosky, A. 1982. *Literacy Before Schooling.* Portsmouth, N.H.: Heinemann.

Neuman, S. B., and Roskos, K. 1990. Play, Print and Purpose: Enriching Play Environments for Literacy Development. *Reading Teacher* 44: 214–21.

Pellegrini, A. D. 1985. Relations Between Preschool Children's Symbolic Play and Literate Behavior. In *Play, Language and Stories,* edited by L. Galda and A. Pellegrini. Norwood, N.J.: Ablex.

Schickedanz, J. A. 1986. *More Than the ABC's: The Early States of Reading and Writing.* Washington, D.C.: National Association for the Education of Young Children.

Schickedanz, J. A.; Hansen, K.; and Forsythe, P. D. 1990. *Understanding Children.* Mountain View, Calif.: Mayfield.

Strickland, D., and Morrow, L. 1989a. Environments Rich in Print Promote Literacy Behavior During Play. *Reading Teacher* 43: 178–79.

Strickland, D., and Morrow, L., eds. 1989b. *Emerging Literacy: Young Children Learn to Read and Write.* Newark, Del.: International Reading Association.

Teale, W., and Sulzby, E., eds. 1986. *Emergent Literacy: Writing and Reading.* Norwood, N.J.: Ablex.

Wells, G. 1986. *The Meaning Makers.* Portsmouth, N.H.: Heinemann.

Chapter 11

THE CHECKLIST CHALLENGE FOR PRIMARY CLASSROOMS

by Alicia Mendoza
and Joyce Rubin

Play is the vehicle of growth, the wheels of movement that allow him to explore the world around him, as well as the adult world of which he will become a part.

—*Jean Piaget*

Play in the primary grades has become as extinct as the dinosaur. The current assumption seems to be that although play is a necessary activity of childhood, it often lures children off the path that leads most directly toward the kind of intellectual growth and success our elementary schools demand. As a result, primary classrooms have become increasingly like their intermediate grade counterparts. They have assumed an air of academic emphasis in the form of long periods of sitting at desks, completing worksheets, listening to instruction, and similar activities more closely associated with the intermediate and upper grades.

Formal academic instruction for six- to eight-year-olds is the antithesis of developmentally appropriate practice; the former does not offer children what they need to achieve optimal development. In fact, current research affirms that children "learn most effectively through a concrete, play-oriented approach" (Bredekamp 1987). Planning a developmentally appropriate curriculum provides the structural base for this approach, and implementation provides for the realization of one's goals and objectives.

The structure and organization of the primary classroom are indeed reflective of the philosophy of how and what children learn during these crucial years. Several factors are observable that

115

reflect the appropriateness of the curriculum. The keen observer can make specific judgments as to whether or not a developmentally appropriate curriculum is being implemented by focusing on the classroom environment, the interrelationships between and among adults and children, and the opportunities for and structure of learning experiences.

The checklist that follows is divided into these three major areas: Physical Environment, Interpersonal Relationships, and Structure of Learning Experiences. It can be used to focus attention on the key components enumerated.

We caution against discouragement if your own classrooms, because of space, time, and other limitations, do not fulfill all the enumerated criteria all the time. Rather, this checklist should serve as motivation to further improve the learning environment of the children you serve. The items it contains are intended to prompt discussion and self-evaluation and to inspire the user to examine settings and programs in terms of environmental, interpersonal, and curricular approaches that may be new, forgotten, or abandoned. This, coupled with continued professional development, should yield promising results in most primary classrooms. In this way, teachers can be ready to do their best for the primary grade child, rather than just expecting the primary grade child to be ready to do the best for them.

Checklist of Primary Classroom Play/Learning Opportunities

PHYSICAL ENVIRONMENT

OCCURS

Usually	Some-times	Rarely	COMPONENT
____	____	____	1. Does the physical environment afford opportunities for various types of play as teaching/learning opportunities?
____	____	____	2. Are seating and classroom floor space use configured and flexible to accommodate differing activities as and when they occur?
____	____	____	3. Are materials to support play-oriented teaching/learning opportunities readily available and presented in an orderly, attractive, and inviting manner that fosters independent accomplishment?
____	____	____	4. Are children with special needs integrated into the classroom, rather than isolated?
____	____	____	5. Are bulletin boards current and reflective of the interests, involvement, and productivity of children?
____	____	____	6. Are noisy and quiet activities distanced from each other so they do not interfere with the teaching/learning opportunities available?
____	____	____	7. Is adequate floor space available for individual work in learning/play centers as well as for small and large group activities?

INTERPERSONAL RELATIONSHIPS

OCCURS

Usually	Some-times	Rarely	COMPONENT
____	____	____	1. Do adults talk and listen to children on a face-to-face level?
____	____	____	2. Are positive interpersonal relationships fostered during individual adult-child experiences as well as small and large group activities?
____	____	____	3. Are peer interaction and support evident through conversation while children work and play daily?
____	____	____	4. Does the teacher promote prosocial behavior, independence, and industry?
____	____	____	5. Are the children motivated toward task completion by building on their intrinsic motivation?
____	____	____	6. Does the teacher model enthusiasm for learning?
____	____	____	7. Does the classroom climate reflect an atmosphere of emotional comfort and security?
____	____	____	8. Is mutual respect evidenced between adults and other adults, children and adults, and children and other children?
____	____	____	9. Do the adults and children seem to enjoy being in each other's company within the classroom setting?

OCCURS

Usually	Some-times	Rarely	Component
____	____	____	10. Are the children encouraged to ask questions, express opinions, and make comments without fear of belittlement and/or negative responses and reactions?
____	____	____	11. Do the adults reinforce and enhance the self-esteem of all the children by fostering success rather than failure?

STRUCTURE OF LEARNING ACTIVITIES

Usually	Some-times	Rarely	COMPONENT
OCCURS			
____	____	____	1. Is there variety in the ways in which learning activities are structured?
____	____	____	2. Does the teacher provide generous amounts of time and activities to facilitate goal fulfillment?
____	____	____	3. Are learning materials and activities concrete and relevant to the lives of the children?
____	____	____	4. Are hands-on activities, rather than worksheets and workbooks, integrated into the daily curriculum?
____	____	____	5. Is higher-level thinking encouraged while rote learning is minimized?
____	____	____	6. Do materials advance from the simple to the complex and from the concrete to the abstract?
____	____	____	7. Are activities designed to enhance children's knowledge and skills in all developmental areas in an integrated manner?
____	____	____	8. Are learning and activity centers used to individualize and integrate learning opportunities?
____	____	____	9. Is a conscious attempt made to use a variety of modalities during instruction?
____	____	____	10. Are the children encouraged to be appropriately physically active during learning activities?

120

STRUCTURE OF LEARNING ACTIVITIES (continued)

OCCURS

Usually	Some-times	Rarely	COMPONENT
____	____	____	11. Is a reasonable level of task-related noise expected and permitted during active play/learning opportunities?
____	____	____	12. Are play/learning opportunities offered to individuals, small and large groups, as appropriate to the needs of the children and the nature of the particular activity?
____	____	____	13. Are the play/learning opportunities used developmentally appropriate to the range of intellectual, physical, and social capabilities of the group?
____	____	____	14. Are children encouraged to develop their independence, creativity, initiative, and curiosity through deliberately planned and executed activities?
____	____	____	15. Does the teacher depart (on occasion) from planned activities and schedules, to take advantage of unplanned incidents or expressions of interest as catalysts for learning?
____	____	____	16. Are activities offered that provide opportunities for self-evaluation, immediate feedback, and self-correction?
____	____	____	17. Are materials at activity centers changed frequently, as appropriate to the changing needs of children?

STRUCTURE OF LEARNING ACTIVITIES (continued)

OCCURS

Usually	Some-times	Rarely	COMPONENT
____	____	____	18. Do children have opportunities to initiate ideas and plans for work and play, with the assurance that adults will help effect them?
____	____	____	19. Are reading, language, and spelling taught as subskills in an integrated manner?
____	____	____	20. Are math and science taught through the use of manipulatives, the discovery approach, and problem-solving experiences?
____	____	____	21. Are social studies and health taught through the use of projects, independent and cooperative learning, and firsthand experiences?
____	____	____	22. Is creative expression through art, music, and movement integrated into the daily program?
____	____	____	23. Is there a multicultural and nonsexist approach to learning?
____	____	____	24. Is evaluation primarily through observation, review of samples of children's work, and recording of individual progress?
____	____	____	25. Are errors viewed as a natural part of learning?

RESOURCES FOR PRIMARY
PROBLEM SOLVERS

Bredekamp, S., ed. 1987. *Developmentally Appropriate Practice in Early Childhood Programs Serving Children from Birth Through Age 8.* Washington, D.C.: National Association for the Education of Young Children.

McGee, L., and Richgeis, D. 1990. *Literacy's Beginnings: Supporting Young Readers and Writers.* Boston: Allyn and Bacon.

Piaget, J. 1970. *Science and Education and the Psychology of the Child.* New York: Orion Press.

———. 1973. *To Understand Is to Invent.* New York: Grossman.

Read, K., and Gardner, R. 1987. *Early Childhood Programs: Human Relationships and Learning.* Fort Worth, Texas: Holt, Rinehart and Winston.

Schickedanz, J., et al. 1990. *Strategies for Teaching Young Children.* Englewood Cliffs, N.J.: Prentice Hall.

Smilansky, S., and Shefatya, L. 1990. *Facilitating Play: A Medium for Promoting Cognitive, Socio-Emotional and Academic Development in Young Children.* Gaithersburg, Md.: Psychosocial and Educational Publications.

Sutton-Smith, B., ed. 1979. *Play and Learning.* New York: Gardner Press.

U.S. Department of Education. 1986. *What Works: Research About Teaching and Learning.* Washington, D.C.: U.S. Government Printing Office.

Wasserman, S. 1990. *Serious Players in the Primary Classroom.* New York: Teachers College Press.

Yawkey, T. D., and Pellegrini, A. D., eds. 1984. *Child's Play: Developmental and Applied.* Hillsdale, N.J.: Erlbaum.

Chapter 12

HELPING THE YOUNG CHILD WITH SCHOOL ADJUSTMENT PROBLEMS

by Charles H. Wolfgang

Four-year-old Jason is the only son of a rugged, athletic, chain-smoking father and an attractive primary school teacher mother. Because of recent moves he has been in and out of a number of early childhood centers, and there is some speculation that he was requested to leave the other centers. Jason is a thin-featured, pale (to the point of looking anemic), tense child who appears as tightly coiled as a spring and rejects any supportive touch by the teacher. Jason never uses the school toilet but often shows many indications of needing to do so, such as holding his stomach and carrying himself as if he is experiencing stomach cramps. He often wets himself during nap time and rarely relaxes or falls asleep.

At lunch or snack time, where he refuses most foods, he seats himself with the more excitable boys and uses bathroom talk in a whispered, covert manner. His words whip the boys into a giggling frenzy that usually ends with their throwing food at each other. When the teacher approaches to stop this behavior, Jason puts down his head, smiles slightly, and acts as if he is totally innocent.

During the classroom play periods he acts like a caged tiger, normally crouching in a protective corner in the block room, wanting to use the materials but not feeling free to do so. His attitude seems to say, "If I start a block structure someone will destroy it." This fearful and untrusting view of his peers causes him to lash out with sharp fingernails, sometimes directly at the other children's eyes, and to repeatedly bite peers for the most minor contact. After his aggression he tells the teacher that the other child was hostile to him; but upon investigation or close observation, it usually turns out that

125

the other child merely bumped him accidentally or inadvertently stepped on one of his toys. He cannot look the teacher directly in the eye, and usually turns away when invited to join activities.

On the rare occasions when he picks Jason up, his father seems impatient to get in and out of the school. Jason complicates matters by refusing to come when called and running to the opposite side of the playground. This causes his father to move after him, forcing the father to play a game of "run and chase." On one occasion when he felt no teacher was looking, the frustrated father struck Jason sharply on the buttocks, and departed dragging a sobbing Jason by the arm. Jason also refuses to permit his mother to leave in the mornings and refuses to reunite or depart with her. She reacts by whispering in his ear about bribes of candy or gifts that she has for him in the car. During conferences his mother refuses to discuss aggressive behavior or adjustment difficulties, changing the topic to his performance in more academic curricula and showing dissatisfaction that the teacher is not teaching him to read.[1]

How should teachers with a Jason in their classrooms—a typical child with adjustment difficulties—view such behavior and what actions should they take to help him?[2] *Children are what they are today because of what they have experienced in their not-so-many yesterdays!*

Jason has gone through the developmental stages of *trust versus mistrust* in the first year of life and *autonomy versus shame and doubt* from ages one to three, and he is currently moving through the stage of *initiative versus guilt* from ages three to seven. According to developmental theorists, behavior, especially that of young children, is as it is because of their early life experiences.[3] Each of the three Eriksonian stages views the child's social-emotional growth as shaped by polar opposites (i.e., trust in contrast to an overdeveloped sense of mistrust). Personality is a series of building blocks added to by each stage, first as a child and then later as an adult, in terms of adjustments. Thus we create a building or structure of our functioning abilities or identity. The young child who demonstrates real adjustment

126

problems in his early childhood classroom needs skilled teachers who understand these developmental stages to formulate a plan of supportive intervention and provide supplemental care giving that can remediate many of the budding difficulties seen in Jason's behavior. Children such as Jason need basic adjustment abilities before they can master later academic and traditional forms of school demands. Young children who have these adjustment skills

- feel comfortable and at ease at key times such as departing and reuniting with parents; eating with others; sleeping or resting; being in a group for circle time; and handling basic toileting needs.
- show control of and skill with using a host of classroom materials to express symbolically their thoughts and feelings.
- give and accept love and affection from both teachers and peers.
- use language to express their needs and feel they have the power to make the world work for them.
- demonstrate social skills as a co-player with peers.

These well-adjusted indicators can be seen as coming to maturity in the expressive play of the young child. From ages three to seven, adjusted children draw fully on all domains of development (i.e., physical, social, cognitive, and emotional) when they experience and express the most advanced form of age-appropriate play, sociodramatic play. This has been defined as

1. Imitative role play
2. Make-believe play with objects
3. Make-believe play with actions and situations
4. Persistence in role play
5. Interaction with others
6. Using language in verbal exchange.[4]

The attainment of highly elaborated, skilled levels of sociodramatic play is an indicator of a fully adjusted child at this age. Thus our ultimate goal for any intervention process to be used with children who have adjustment difficulties will be to lead them to the maturity level that enables them to enact and sustain sociodramatic play.[5] The child who cannot play, such as Jason, does not possess a developmentally solid personality structure that will make academic achievement in the primary grades possible; such a child requires the teacher's intervention.[6]

TRUST VERSUS MISTRUST

In his past experiences Jason acquired a "life stance position or view of his world"[7]—of mistrust—which is still developing. He experiences and then perceives that others, such as peers or even his mother and father, are not dependable, and may even be the source of physical pain. The young infant experiences the new world through repetitive, early, very basic encounters focusing around bodily needs such as physical warmth and feeding. From the outside world comes the physical care of his body, being cuddled, held, and "bathed" with physical and verbal affection. This basic sense of trust will be channeled from the outside caring world through the child's modalities or the senses of touch, taste, smell, and vision. These same senses can be "punished," however, and become channels that bring pain and fear, resulting in mistrust. In any assessment of young children, therefore, we may ask such questions as those that follow.

1. *Can he/she cuddle?* (touch) Does the child accept our physical platonic embrace as affection after a positive experience, such as successfully completing a difficult puzzle? Or can he accept comfort after a negative one, such as a playground fall? Can the child use the teacher as an "emotional gas station,"[8] acquiring emotional energy through cuddling with the teacher, then returning to daily school activities with renewed energy? Or, is physical touching from adults rejected as if touch will hurt and give pain? Jason perceives touch of any type as a potentially hurting overture from others. Our body should be a pleasurable modality to experience our world; children like Jason show by

their rejection of touch that, at the body level, experiences have weighed them down with *mistrust*.

2. *How does he/she eat at meals or snack time?* (taste) Eating is "being given to by others," especially in early care giving. It is one of the first acts from others that develops feelings in the child that the world is dependable. This "being given to" is the genesis of early attachment[9] to others and the genesis of *trust* that others will help maintain an inner balance of "pleasurableness," or the feeling of being well cared for. Later this attachment or bonding process will incorporate others such as siblings and peers. We may continue to view eating together as a bonding process even in adulthood, as we invite friends or those we wish to influence to join us for food: "Let's do lunch." The Norman Rockwell view of family clustered around the Thanksgiving table is a classic metaphor for acceptance and belonging. When children such as Jason refuse to eat in a community of others and even act out to disrupt these social experiences, we may interpret this behavior as another expression of a lack of basic *trust*.

3. *How does he/she relate to adults and peers in nonverbal manners?* (vision) A child's feelings of acceptance are signaled nonverbally by physically turning toward the teacher as the person to whom she wishes to give and accept affection; this is usually accompanied by eye contact and a smile. Dropping the eyes when others wish to communicate, refusing to participate in play with others, and defensive positioning in corners of the block room as a protective stance—all combine to suggest a pattern or life stance toward others that shows Jason's basic feeling of *mistrust*. Dropping the eyes or refusing to look at another may be characterized as "punished vision," or the fear that to look in the face of adults might be punished.[10]

Hearing is a sense modality that can also be punished. This can be observed when a child responds by covering his ears with his hands, by turning away and showing fear and perhaps crying, as "not wanting to hear" noises and sounds that are normal and not disrupting to other children (e.g., male voices or voices of adult authorities). "Punished hearing" can also be seen in children who have been verbally chastised excessively.

A parent picking up her four-year-old son at the end of the day stated, "I'm not going to put your jacket on! You are a big boy now, you know how to put this on!" While chastising the child, the mother was gently putting his arm into the sleeve of his jacket. Her words, in the form of "friendly" chastising (not seen on the surface as negative by the teacher) were the opposite of her actions with the child. The child tuned out listening to his mother's words because they were not connected to the real actions occurring. When teachers first worked with this child, he appeared deaf, seeming not to hear directions, greetings, and verbal overtures easily understood by all the other children. When he was checked by a specialist, no hearing loss was found. The child had acquired "punished hearing"; he appeared to have turned off listening to the voices of others that he had learned were chastising and contradicted real action.

AUTONOMY VERSUS SHAME AND DOUBT

During the second year of life, children move through the stage of autonomy versus shame and doubt. At this time, when they are able to walk and be spatially independent of early care givers, they actively begin to assert themselves, to "be the cause" in their world. These attempts are of course built on the amount of trust they have previously developed. Autonomy suggests that maturing toddlers start to act on their world of other people and toys and materials, beginning a process of gaining self-control over their self-centered wishes—"I want what I want when I want it, and I wanted it yesterday."

Doubt and shame come when adult care givers set limits and make demands on the child's self-control of body and actions so that the toddler cannot always get what he wants when he wants it. For example, sleeping, eating, and toileting are under the control of the child, but during this period controlling adults make demands for going to bed in a timely manner, eating in a controlled, sensible manner, and toileting in an adult manner. Thus these points become areas for autonomy struggles between the child and adults, and conflicts are brought into and seen in the classroom. As a result, questions are asked about the child's adjustment behavior:

- How does the child depart and reunite with parents?
- How does the child rest at nap time?
- How does the child "potty" himself or herself?

In Jason's case we see negative adjustment in each of these areas. He uses a run-and-chase behavior to control his parents when reuniting, rarely sleeps, and often makes noises that disturb others. He refuses the school toilet even when it is obvious that he needs to use it and wets his cot at nap time. There is much evidence of doubt, holding on to, a need for control, and an inability to be at ease in these key classroom times and activities. Like a toddler, he is constantly fighting for his own place within a preschool group where others are ready for the cooperative joys of playing together.

INITIATIVE VERSUS GUILT

Ages three to seven are the stage of initiative versus guilt when children want to do as adults do. New creative ideas lead to attempts to initiate a host of actions, to test themselves with and against adults and peers. Guilt grows, however, when their actions overstep the bounds of family values and they "fail" to live up to adult demands. It is during these years that, with sufficient basic trust, autonomy, and initiative, the child will become secure enough to develop abilities to participate in social actions as an equal. At the end of this stage, the child has obtained the social-emotional strength to inhibit the desire to hoard and destroy, and can carry out agreed-upon goals and activities with others, thus becoming a cooperative worker at the age of "formal" schooling. The abilities to take part in sociodramatic play and to use school materials to construct and create products in painting, clay, block building, puzzles, etc., help children like Jason become fully adjusted participants, ready to benefit from the teacher's guidance and the school's curriculum.

A PROGRAM OF INTERVENTION

To help children like Jason in the classroom, teachers must evaluate their behavior in terms of the questions previously suggested and then provide a series of supportive actions to help reestablish basic trust and reawaken feelings of autonomy and initiative. This may take many days, even months. During this age, however, children are still formulating basic personality characteristics, and teachers can make important contributions to their development. Following are a limited number of supportive or helping techniques that may be used to help these children. This intervention process will generally require three steps: (1) reestablishing basic trust in the teacher as a helping adult; (2) providing parameters that enable the child to feel free to practice autonomy with materials but also with control; and (3) initiating creative use of materials and play with others.

Helping Techniques

Trust in Teachers

The movement from a home setting to a school setting presents a form of cultural shock to the young child much like that of an adult who quickly moves from a well-known community to a foreign country. When young children show stress by demanding that parents not leave, they cry and wish to hold on to the parents; this behavior evidences positive attachment between parent and child, love and basic trust in the parents. This trust needs to *extend* to the teacher and classroom adults. Normally it goes through three phases: lap phase with customs inspection, practicing phase, and teacher approach phase.

Lap Phase with Customs Inspection. Three-year-old Kate enters the classroom door, tightly holding her mother's hand. After child and parent are warmly greeted by the teacher, silently observed by the other children, the full meaning of going to school and leaving mother begins to come to Kate. She climbs on her mother's lap and buries her face in her mother's chest. For a few minutes she refuses to look at this new world. The teacher encourages the mother to take the rocking chair to a large upright mirror mounted on the wall, and suggests that when Kate feels more relaxed, her mother might demonstrate some of the toys to her. Then the teacher leaves, saying she will be back shortly to help.

Next, we see Kate stop crying and begin peeking over her mother's shoulder to watch the classroom activities through the mirror. She begins pointing things out to her mother, and the two chat about what is happening. (This is the customs inspection period.)

Practicing Phase. After looking about the room for a while, Kate suddenly slips from her mother's lap, runs out into the classroom to grab a toy, and brings it quickly back to her mother. Then, standing at her mother's knee, she watches to see if anyone will intervene—making eye contact with the teacher. The teacher smiles and communicates by looking and smiling that it is OK.

"Oh, this is a toy dog," Mother says. "It goes 'ruff-ruff' and walks like this." Three or four times Kate runs out, grabs an object, darts back, and puts it in her mother's hands; her mother responds by telling her the name of the object and demonstrating its uses. (In this practicing phase the child is practicing spatial separation from the parent for short periods.)[11]

We noticed that the teacher did not throw herself at the child, but permitted the child and parent time to relax and gradually physically separate. During the gradual separation the teacher was observing the parent-child interaction, noting the sense modalities used by the mother:

- Hearing—Is the mother trying to reassure the child by using language to explain: "This is what we are doing, this is what will happen next, etc."? (If so, she may be a verbal mother.)

- Touch—Is the mother cuddling and caressing the child, as well as exploring objects with her own hands and encouraging the child to do likewise? (She may be a tactile mother.)

133

- Visual—Is the mother signaling the child with her eyes, telling her to go ahead and pick up the object, just by using her eyes and facial expressions? (She may be a visual mother.)

Teacher Approach Phase. From her careful observations of mother-child interaction, the teacher has just learned something about the sense modalities that she may now use to make this child begin to feel comfortable in her new classroom world. For the hearing-verbal child, the teacher talks with the child about what is happening or going to happen ("We are going to read a book about . . . You will sit near me so that you may hear the story."). For the tactile-physical child, the teacher brings a furry puppet, or takes the child to the classroom rabbit, encouraging her to touch, and to learn the classroom world through touch. For the visual child, the teacher may signal with her eyes that there is a free chair, toy, or materials available and encourage the child visually to use them. With an understanding of the child's strong modality, the teacher can now communicate with this child, becoming an organizer and an anchor of trust.

The teacher starts to intervene to help the child establish trust, use autonomy, and initiate play and cooperative actions with peers. Thus the child can begin to give and accept love and affection from both teacher and peers and to feel comfortable and at ease at key times such as departing and reuniting with parents, eating with others, sleeping or resting, being in a group for circle time, and handling basic toileting needs. Let us take one example of children attempting to meet the goal of using language to express their needs and feel that they have the power to make the world work for them and demonstrate social skills as co-players with peers.

Gaining Trust to Play
and Work with Peers

The conflicts between Jason and his peers are valuable incidents to help him develop the skill to gain autonomy and power to play and work with other children in the classroom, and to feel secure and confident in doing so. Jason has found a shovel

Figure 1
Teacher Behavioral Continuum (TBC)

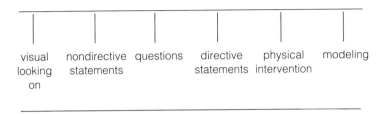

visual looking on   nondirective statements   questions   directive statements   physical intervention   modeling

Source: Charles H. Wolfgang and Mary E. Wolfgang, *School for Young Children: Developmentally Appropriate Play Curriculum and Practices for Teaching Children Three to Five* (Boston: Allyn and Bacon, 1991).

in the sandbox and is just about to fill a bucket. Mark, seated nearby, has a bucket but no shovel. Mark takes Jason's shovel and Jason starts to attack. The teacher's goal is to help Jason use language to express his needs and feel that he has the power to make the world work for him.

The teacher begins by bringing the two children together either at a private corner of the sandbox or by simply holding one hand of each child and bringing them face to face. Now the adult looks on, allowing time for the children to try to settle their argument without further teacher intervention. The target is Jason because he has the immediate problem—he lost his shovel. Jason can respond in a number of nonproductive ways: being passive—just leaving or surrendering the toy; being physically aggressive—striking out or biting Mark; or being verbally aggressive—calling Mark names, swearing, etc. But the goal is to resolve social conflict through impulse control and expressive language. So if Jason does not control and express himself, the teacher escalates intervention to more intrusive behavior on a construct called the Teacher Behavioral Continuum (TBC). (See Figure 1.)

If Jason does not assert himself with the use of language, the helping teacher moves up the TBC to nondirective statements: "Jason, I can see by your face that you are unhappy; you have lost your shovel." The teacher has "verbally encoded" both Jason's feelings (much like active listening),[12] and the problem.

If there is no reaction from Jason, the teacher escalates to the question strategy: "Jason, what could you say to Mark?" Then she retreats to visually looking to give Jason some time to think and respond. If he still does not react, the teacher moves to directive statements: "Tell Mark what you want." After a period of wait-time, the helping adult moves to modeling: "Tell Mark, no, that is my shovel. I was using it. I want it back!"

At this point, if Jason does not respond, the teacher might say: "You are having a difficult time using words with Mark. Would you like me to tell him for you this time?" If he indicates yes, the teacher repeats the language modeling directly to Mark: "Mark, Jason wants me to tell you that he was using the shovel and wants you to give it back to him." The experienced teacher will do this for the child only once. From that time on, the teacher will continue using the TBC techniques, but after verbal modeling he or she will simply leave, telling and helping the child to learn to use language to get what he needs.

Some teachers feel that this reaction is unfair and that Mark is getting away with something, but there will be many other occasions to deal with Mark. Right now Jason needs a lesson in asserting himself with language. If the teacher relieves Jason of stress, getting what he needs for him, the child will have no need to learn to act autonomously. If the adult's overdeveloped sense of fairness pushes the teacher to play judge and jury, returning all objects to "rightful" owners, she will be continuously exhausted because all the children will be pulling at her clothes to settle numerous conflicts daily. Rather, when clashes over possessions occur, the experienced teacher will continue to intervene using the TBC scale technique, until one day Jason will assert himself and gain the power to use language in the context of conflict. There can be no more valuable lesson.

Backtracking a bit, if Jason *does* respond or simply says, "No, stop, that is mine!" the target child becomes Mark. Mark must learn to respond to the language of peers, and adults may teach him this by using the steps on the TBC. First, the teacher simply looks on as the children stand face to face, giving Mark time to think and return the item. If he is unable to do so, the teacher would move to nondirective statements, questions, directive statements, and physical intervention or modeling. With the ability to manage social conflicts through language, children such as Jason can now develop through the social stages[13] leading to their becoming sociodramatic players and eventually cooperative workers.

The important thing to understand in this conflict management strategy is that teachers have an orderly method of intervention through the use of the Teacher Behavioral Continuum. This method attains the goal of establishing within children a feeling of trust in themselves that they can become autonomous in handling interactions with their peers by initiating actions through language to maintain their power. Similar structuring or organizing by the teacher will also be needed to meet the remaining goals of feeling comfortable and at ease at key times (departing and reuniting with parents; eating with others; sleeping or resting; being in a group for circle time; and handling basic toileting needs), and showing control of and skill with classroom materials to express thoughts and feelings symbolically. As Jason gains skill and competence in each area, his nonproductive and aggressive behaviors decrease dramatically. Day by day he becomes a child ready to play and, increasingly, ready to learn from his teachers and his peers.

In the following chapter, Carbonara and Scanlon provide a picture of classroom and therapeutic intervention that conveys the complexity of the intervention process. They show the levels of intervention addressed here and the mutually reinforcing work of teacher and therapist helping a young girl with psychological problems.

NOTES

[1]Adapted from Charles H. Wolfgang and Mary E. Wolfgang, *School for Young Children: Developmentally Appropriate Play Curriculum and Practices for Teaching Children Three to Five* (Boston: Allyn and Bacon, 1991).

[2]The data in our example might suggest that actions with, toward, or on Jason's mother and father might be required, but that would be the topic of another chapter. Here we focus on our sphere of action within the classroom and directly with Jason.

[3]Erikson, E., *Childhood and Society,* 2d ed. (New York: Norton, 1950).

[4]Smilansky, S., and L. Shefatya, *Facilitating Play: A Medium for Promoting Cognitive, Socio-Emotional and Academic Development in Young Children* (Gaithersburg, Md.: Psychosocial and Educational Publications, 1990).

[5]See the following writings for a fuller explanation of sociodramatic play and its value to development: Singer, Jerome L., *The Child's World of Make-Believe: Experimental Studies of Imaginative Play* (New York: Academic Press, 1973); Smilansky, S., and L. Shefatya, *Facilitating Play.*

[6]When the word "adjustment" is used, we are referring to those problem children found in nearly every classroom, but who are considered within the broad range of "normal" children. A pathological child would be outside the sphere of teacher abilities and these suggestions.

[7]Berne, Eric, *Games People Play: The Psychology of Human Relations* (New York: Grove Press, 1964).

[8]Mahler, M. S., *On Human Symbiosis and the Vicissitudes of Individuation* (New York: International Universities Press, 1970); Mahler, M. S. et al., *The Psychological Birth of the Human Infant* (New York: Basic Books, 1975); Mahler, M. S., and LaPerriere, K., "Mother-Child Interaction During Separation-Individuation," *Psychoanalytical Quarterly* 21, no. 34 (1954): 483–98.

[9]Mahler, M. S. et al., *The Psychological Birth of the Human Infant;* Spitz, R. A., *The First Year of Life* (New York: International Universities Press, 1957).

[10]One must also realize that some cultural groups use a similar dropping of eyes as a form of respect and this should not be viewed as problematic. The teacher would need to place this behavior in context

with a host of other indicators of adjustment.

[11]Speers, R. W., *Variations in Separation-Individuation and Implications for Play Ability and Learning as Studies in the Three-Year-Old in Nursery School* (Pittsburgh: University of Pittsburgh Press, 1970).

[12]Gordon, T., *TET: Teacher Effectiveness Training* (New York: McKay, 1974).

[13]Parten, M. B., "Social Play Among Preschool Children." In *Child's Play,* edited by R. E. Herron and B. Sutton-Smith (New York: Wiley, 1971), 83–95.

Chapter 13

FACILITATING PLAY WITH YOUNG CHILDREN AT RISK: A CASE STUDY

by Nancy Trevorrow Carbonara
and Paula Scanlon

Dolores was the younger of two girls in a divorced family. She was just three when her mother sought therapeutic help. Dolores attended nursery school two days a week, but was on the verge of being expelled because of tantrums when she was expected to adhere to school routines or teacher-established limits in play or outdoor activities. At other times during the school day, she seemed withdrawn, engaged in solitary play, and was termed a loner. Her mother reported a similar pattern at home: she was cooperative on some days, extremely oppositional on others, seemed unsociable, and withdrew to her room more frequently than her mother considered normal. Her mother also was concerned about Dolores's poorly articulated speech and her habit of running away when they were in public.

When the therapist first met Dolores, her mother had to carry her into the session; at the end of the session she bolted and ran away from her mother, out of the building, and into the parking lot. During her session she spoke very little. Her speech was immature, hard to understand, and poorly articulated. The first thing she touched in the room was a baby bottle. She explored toys in a thoughtful manner, but kept returning to the bottle, finally asking to have it filled with water and sucking on it lustily—almost ecstatically. She was able to pretend to feed a doll for a few moments, then returned to feeding herself. Other brief bits of symbolic play in which she engaged seemed to indicate that, besides feeling greatly in need of furtherance, Dolores was concerned about being "bad," worried about body injury, and experienced intense conflict about regressing to infancy or growing up. The therapist hypothesized that her behavior pattern of extreme rebellion alternating with extreme withdrawal represented the only ways she had developed for managing overwhelming anxiety, including separation anxiety.

Speech did not seem to be a comfortable mode of expression for this child, but it seemed possible that play could be. A focus in therapy was helping her move from direct acting out, such as sucking the bottle and tantrums, to expressing herself in symbolic play and art. Her growing ability to use those forms of expression emerged as a significant strength.

Dolores was able to modify her behavior enough to remain in nursery school, but became even more difficult at home. She repeated nursery school in the three-year-old class. At the end of that year she was tested to determine whether she was ready for kindergarten. Since the school she would enter provided an unusually sensitive environment for young children, it seemed likely that she could benefit from that program and the decision was made for her transition from private nursery to public kindergarten.

The kindergarten Dolores attended is part of a suburban public school district. The curriculum is play-based and sessions are two and a half hours long. Dolores attended the morning session and was one of the youngest, both chronologically and developmentally, in a class of 18 children.

Dolores began the kindergarten year by participating in activities in a rather low-keyed, serious manner. She regularly chose to work in the art and manipulative areas where she engaged mostly in solitary play. She had the basic verbal and social skills necessary to communicate with peers to share materials and play spaces. During the first weeks of school, she also participated in group activities, discussions, and routines.

Toward the end of the morning during the sixth week of school, her quiet participation changed rather abruptly when the children were working on individual collages. While cutting and gluing, Dolores began eating the glue. This behavior occurred the following day and was accompanied by attempts to disrupt her peers: pulling at laces and papers, dripping water on people, and scribbling on their papers.

This disruptive behavior occurred over a two-week period, always during the last, most structured, and group-oriented part of the morning. A multidisciplinary team was used to develop strategies for evaluation and intervention. The school nurse consulted with Dolores's mother to determine whether any physical issues were involved. Throughout the second week during independent work time, the principal made herself available in the room. She helped Dolores regain control when necessary and then encouraged her attempts to finish the art projects.

Dolores's mother also gave the teacher permission to consult with the child's therapist. In these discussions the teacher highlighted the strengths Dolores had evidenced thus far in the year during free-play activities, including her ability to organize materials and ideas, express herself creatively, interact positively with the teacher and peers, and work purposefully for sustained periods of time. The teacher expressed concern that while Dolores obviously had the skills necessary to complete more structured art projects, her disruptive behavior was an indication that she was not ready to work in this manner.

As a result of her conversation with the therapist, the teacher continued to support Dolores's growth through play and to make adaptations for her participation in more structured work. The teacher encouraged such participation and expected Dolores to sit with her peers; however, when she did not complete or attempt a project, she was allowed to color or rest. After the ninth week of school, she rarely disrupted her peers.

Over the course of the year, Dolores's play grew more flexible and sustained. By spring she would, on occasion, venture into the dramatic play area, mostly taking on a mothering role in interactions with others. Dolores was also formally evaluated by the school district in the spring. As a result of these tests, observations, and discussions with her mother and therapist, Dolores moved on to first grade in the fall, where she continued to grow with the help of flexible teachers and supportive services.

When she entered second grade, Dolores and her family moved to another school district. She continued to have a difficult time academically, particularly in learning to read, but teachers uniformly praised her hard work and good behavior. She related well to peers. At home and in therapy sessions, she continued to erupt into episodes of uncontrolled behavior, but they became less frequent and she recovered more quickly. Times of withdrawal were rare.

Treatment ended when Dolores was nearly nine and had completed third grade. Her academic skills, including reading, were at grade level. Her anxiety had lessened considerably, she clearly wanted to grow up, and her internal psychological organization seemed much sturdier. She was using speech very effectively to communicate socially as well as in therapy sessions.

Through the years, Dolores's play and artwork had become increasingly rich. At the end of treatment both appeared to remain as important resources in her struggles to attain self-control and mastery of emotional conflicts; both also continued to serve her well in expressing her considerable creativity and in strengthening her self-esteem.

Chapter 14

GETTING SERIOUS ABOUT PLAY

by Thomas Schultz

American parents and professionals who work with children are bombarded with advice, analysis, and criticism on every possible aspect of our lives. From the prenatal period through adult relationships with aging parents, families have the sometimes dubious benefit of rafts of manuals, seminars, television discussion hours, video and cassette tapes, and commercial products to guide us when we are uncertain, instruct us when we are inexperienced—and even correct us when we feel confident. Similarly, our public schools and early childhood agencies are awash with analysts and reformers. It is never quite clear whether these helper-critics make a direct impact on how children are raised and instructed, but the social habit continues. So it is with the phenomenon of children's play. This seemingly innocuous, everyday, unremarkable activity has been the subject of expensive, sophisticated research and lively opinionated debate. My purpose in this chapter is to briefly summarize and assess three major strands of criticism and advocacy about children's play:

- *In schools:* Efforts to implement "playful" approaches to teaching and learning in preschool and primary education as a means to promote cognitive development and academic achievement;
- *In communities:* Advocacy for the expansion of child care services, in part to provide a safe, stimulating environment for children's play; and
- *At home:* Initiatives to influence the content of play itself by discouraging violent, competitive, and otherwise undesirable forms of entertainment and recreation.

IN SCHOOLS: DEVELOPMENTALLY APPROPRIATE TEACHING AND PLAY

Play and learning have a complicated relationship—one examined in almost every chapter in this monograph. In the most general sense they are seen as mutually exclusive categories, as in "All work and no play makes Jack a dull boy" or "After you've done your homework you can play." From another aspect, early childhood professionals have long cited the adage "Play is a child's work" and argued that play contributes to the overall development of children and to their ability to learn. They cite evidence that certain forms of play develop problem solving, divergent thinking, language and literacy, and social skills—all valuable parts of learning (Rogers and Sawyers 1988, 56–68).

In the current climate of public opinion, however, we castigate our children and young people for watching too much television, spending too much time playing Nintendo, and neglecting the virtues of homework and reading. Part of the blame for our nation's relatively low performance in educational achievement is laid at the door of these habits. A primary tenet of educational reforms in the 1980s is the view that children need to work harder at academic learning, and that teachers must be motivated to assert higher standards for student work and effort. Increased course requirements, a longer school day and a longer school year, and more "high-stakes" testing to motivate teachers and administrators are all examples of this policy trend. Similarly, research on effective schools promotes an image of a unified staff working toward high achievement on common academic goals, much homework and testing, and tough but fair discipline. As one author suggested, there's almost an underlying Calvinist Protestant ideal that children should be working so hard that "it looks as if it hurts" (Erickson 1986, 144).

While many of these reforms are aimed primarily at secondary school students, these policies have also trickled down into elementary schools and early childhood programs. Observers note that classrooms are increasingly dominated by drill-and-practice activities, use of worksheets and workbooks, teacher-directed, whole-group instruction, and work on discrete skills and bits of knowledge. In response, the early childhood community has launched a counterattack regarding desirable teaching for young children. The National Association for the Education of Young Children's (NAEYC) position statement on developmentally appropriate practice for children birth through age eight (Bredekamp 1987) argues that high-pressure teaching, an emphasis on increased scores on standardized achievement tests, and defining learning as memorizing facts are counterproductive tendencies. More effective teaching for young children should emphasize activities and techniques that are congruent with children's play in many respects:

- Learning through active rather than passive activities
- Learning through concrete experiences rather than via textbooks and workbooks
- Learning through cooperation and dialogue rather than individualized and competitive modes
- Learning that integrates skills and subjects rather than in separate segments by curriculum area
- Learning that encourages individual autonomy and choice rather than dependence on teacher direction.

In response to this agenda, two points of clarification are in order. First, while some criticism by early childhood advocates is directed at inappropriate, overly rigid expectations for academic performance by young children, the claim is that developmentally appropriate methods will lead to positive academic outcomes. Indeed, these forms of activities and teaching are also widely endorsed by groups seeking to improve student learning in different curriculum areas. For example, guidelines from the National Council of Teachers of Mathematics (NCTM) emphasize use of concrete materials and cooperative problem solving in early elementary mathematics and reduced emphasis on worksheets and memorization of facts. (Chapter 8 in this volume also conveys this argument.) Similarly, several groups aiming to improve science education advocate hands-on experiments and projects as opposed to teacher lectures and reliance on textbooks. Second, this agenda will not make schooling effortless, captivating, or as entertaining as a vacation at Disney World.

However, the developmental orientation seems to fit particularly well with aspirations for intellectual curiosity and creativity as ultimate ends. When we think of outstanding scientists, writers, and other professionals, we look for creative, critical, innovative minds rather than speed and accuracy in repeating a canon of facts and knowledge. We value minds that can "play with" ideas, make new connections, pose significant problems, and the like. The enhancement of these attributes does not square with a mechanical, factory-like approach to education. If the child is imbued with undue reverence for given facts, theories, and teachers' explanations, the disposition to critique, analyze, and create new questions and connections may be retarded or subdued.

IN COMMUNITIES:
PLAY AND CHILD CARE

Play used to be viewed as an unplanned, informal activity that absorbed the waking hours of children in the home. We assumed that parents were available to adjudicate disputes and administer first aid or refreshments, and that most of the time children figured out what to do and did it. These days, children's play takes place in very different environments. There are more single-parent families, fewer siblings, more working parents, and a heightened sensitivity to risks to child safety. And parents and other neighborhood residents are less available to exercise informal oversight over play.

Today's parents, then, are caught in a series of dilemmas in providing safe, supervised settings in which their children can play and develop. Working parents search for child care arrangements for their preschool children and supervision for their older children. Increasingly, families of all income levels are choosing organized group care settings to meet this need. As a result, many public schools are organizing to provide varying forms of child care. In the main, child care centers and after-school care programs promote a productive play environment as their primary function. It seems clear that the risks of unsafe and unsupervised or otherwise abysmal-quality child care are too great to ignore. At a policy level, we need to work as hard as possible to eradicate situations where children must take care of themselves or each other—as well as arrangements where untrained adults are attempting to cope with too many children. The risks to physical safety, as well as the anxiety and stress on children in those settings, are substantial.

But I also want to point out what I see as another consequence of this gradual social movement toward organized child care. At home parents are sufficiently available to protect and encourage the child, but there is rarely self-consciously programmatic intent in the air; in child care settings—even when staff are attuned to the values of play—there may be a tendency for staff-initiated, group activities to prevail. Simply because of the presence of many other children and a staff of adults, there may be a bent toward active, engaging group activities. These are fun and productive, but an exclusive diet of this type of play may be less than ideal. What may be missing for children in child care centers are opportunities for privacy, individual activity, and "down time." There should also be a delicate balance between responsible staff oversight and the need for children to be free to explore, to invent activities, and to work out relationships with each other without unnecessary adult intervention.

In summary, we have a major challenge to contend with in building an affordable system to meet child care needs of working parents and to provide safe environments for children's play. As we work to build this infrastructure in schools and other community settings, we need to be sensitive to training staff and designing space that allows for a full range of types of play. And I would argue that a particular dilemma exists between the instincts of active, conscientious child care staff and the need for some aspects of play to be private, child-initiated, and child-regulated.

AT HOME: "GOOD" PLAY
VERSUS "BAD" PLAY

To further complicate matters, early childhood professionals have an agenda for reforming play itself. Active campaigns to reduce violence in television and other media aimed at children, discouraging war toys, arguing against young children participating in highly competitive team sports—all are part of the atmosphere of professional meetings and publications. David Elkind's book *The Hurried Child* typifies this form of advice. It argues that premature exposure to symbols, clothing, activities, and expectations from the world of adults and older children is creating damaging stress for young children. In another recent example, NAEYC's position statement on media violence points out alarming evidence of trends in media aimed at children (e.g., air time for war cartoons increasing from one and a half hours a week in 1982 to 43 hours a week in 1986) and links between heavy viewing of television violence and reduced sensitivity to pain and suffering of others, heightened fearfulness, and increased tendencies toward aggressive behavior among children.

By contrast, early childhood experts nod approvingly at block building, music, and creative artwork, and field trips and projects that explore the natural environment. Watching cartoons and playing Nintendo are frowned upon. "Good play" is reading to your child, going to the zoo, water and sand play, and carpentry. "Bad play" is competitive, violent, discriminatory, preoccupied with inappropriate forms of fantasy, etc.

Improving the quality of play at home involves influencing the same parents who are pressed for time and on limited budgets in their search for child care. One might hope that parents who, in comparison to past generations, have less time to spend with their children would be eager to engage in high-quality, developmentally sound activities. Parents' abilities to set wholesome standards for play demand both physical and emotional energy, however. When parents and children are exhausted by their daily schedules, fast food may win out over more nutritious, "made-from-scratch" meals, and television may win out over more engaging, healthier, but more demanding, forms of play.

PROSPECTS FOR IMPROVEMENT

I have sketched out three major agendas related to children's play. First, in schools, a promising direction for improving teaching and learning involves adaptation of attributes of children's play in classroom activities and pedagogy. Second, improving the quality and affordability of child care is a priority in providing safe environments for children's play. But I have urged sensitivity to providing children with opportunities to create their own activities and solve their own social conflicts (albeit often imperfectly), as well as opportunities for privacy, which may be difficult to satisfy in many child care situations. Third, I have outlined a set of concerns regarding the quality and content of children's play in the home.

Each of these agendas faces a unique set of challenges. Promoting developmentally appropriate practice requires changing the habits and routines of thousands of classroom teachers. Different curricular goals, classroom organization strategies, and learning materials and equipment are required. Policies for teacher evaluation and student assessment need to be changed. School administrators and parents must become accustomed to classrooms that are noisier, more active, less visibly under the direct authority of teachers, and more attuned to individual and group play/learning opportunities.

By contrast, the challenge in improving prospects for play within child care is at a more primitive level today. Simply creating safe spaces with competent adult supervision on a basis affordable to parents is a daunting challenge. Shifting priorities for public funding and building a stable work force are large-scale difficulties. In addition, work is needed to shift public attitudes on core beliefs regarding parental responsibility and the consequences of early experiences in human development. Our present public policies regarding child care may well reflect a broad popular belief that society should not intervene in or

151

support parents in child-rearing prior to the onset of formal public education.

Finally, promoting healthy habits in children's play at home involves efforts to influence very different audiences: corporations marketing products and influencing the media, and parents as consumers. Thus efforts need to address both the supply side and the demand side of the children's play market. It is to be hoped that the increasing involvement of corporate leaders in support of quality early childhood programs will also lead to improvements in private sector product development and marketing, or a regulatory role by government may be the most useful lever for change. Strategies for influencing parents may begin with public education regarding the importance of play, but they also may need to extend to improving overall supports for the family—financial assistance, parental leave, part-time and flex-time work schedules, and greater symbolic credit for parents who play a constructive role in their children's play.

Thus challenges in improving prospects for children's play in schools, community settings, and homes will require concerted action at the policy level and in the daily activities of teachers, care givers, and parents.

REFERENCES

Bredekamp, S., ed. 1987. *Developmentally Appropriate Practice in Early Childhood Programs Serving Children from Birth Through Age 8.* Washington, D.C.: National Association for the Education of Young Children.

Elkind, D. 1981. *The Hurried Child: Growing Up Too Fast Too Soon.* Reading, Mass.: Addison-Wesley.

Erickson, F. 1986. Tasks in Times: Objects of Study in a Natural History of Teaching. In *Improving Teaching: 1986 ASCD Yearbook,* edited by K. Zumwalt, 131–47. Alexandria, Va.: Association for Supervision and Curriculum Development.

————. July 1990. NAEYC Position Statement on Media Violence in Children's Lives. *Young Children,* 18–21.

Rogers, C., and Sawyers, J. 1988. *Play in the Lives of Children.* Washington, D.C.: National Association for the Education of Young Children.

Chapter 15

PLAY'S PLACE IN TEACHER EDUCATION

by Stephanie Feeney

As this book demonstrates so well, there is today great consensus regarding the value of play in children's development among child development researchers and early childhood educators in the field. Play is well known as a vehicle for ongoing intellectual, physical, social, and emotional growth and development. This growth can be aided by teachers who are sensitive to children's needs, interests, and developmental stages. Through their attitudes and their actions, teachers have a powerful influence on the depth and nature of young children's play, and teachers have a significant role in supporting or discouraging the types of productive play discussed in this monograph in their classrooms.

Despite everything that we know of its value, play is not prevalent in the great majority of our nation's classrooms for young children, especially in those educating five- to eight-year-olds. Several contributors to the excellent new book *Children's Play and Learning* discuss the reasons why play is so poorly supported in early childhood education settings:

1. Teachers are only superficially aware of the value of play, or understand only its role in social and emotional and not intellectual development. Because of their hazy or incomplete understanding, they are unable to defend it to parents and administrators.

2. Teachers are not accustomed to seeking out the research base for their practice, nor do they know how to translate research into practice. Therefore even if they read research on play, they are unlikely to act upon it.

155

3. In our society, a much higher status is accorded to work than to play, and this leads to the view that play is frivolous and not to be taken seriously in educational settings.

4. The pressure for early academics and the emphasis on standardized tests have led to the "pushing down" of the elementary curriculum into kindergarten and "pre-kindergarten" classrooms, which have become very much like the first and second grade classrooms of the past. When "academic" learning is emphasized and defined as primarily paper-pencil activity, play is regarded as a luxury to be engaged in only after serious "work" is completed. (Monighan-Nourot 1990; Kagan 1990; Smilansky 1990)

PLAY AND TEACHER EDUCATION

Sara Smilansky writes that there is a great need to promote play: "Basic attitudes clearly need changing. . . . The most appropriate forums for making needed changes in attitudes are the teacher preparation institutions" (1990, 40). If play is to occur in early childhood classrooms, teacher training programs must help people entering the field to recognize its importance and learn to provide worthwhile play experiences for young children.

Yet Barbara Bowman says in her chapter "Play in Teacher Education: The United States Perspective":

In view of the dominant role of play in theory and practice, one would expect it to be a significant aspect of teacher education. A sample of college catalogues suggests this is not the case. Colleges list few courses entitled "Play," and in most, the word play does not even appear in course descriptions. Professional standards also fail to mention play as an essential aspect of teachers' competency. Its emphasis in teacher education is often less than one would expect considering its importance in development. (1990, 97–98)

Bowman points out that play is often included in college catalogs under topics like creative activities, choosing toys and materials, and designing learning environments. The fact that the word *play* is so rarely used may mean that even early childhood educators believe that it is a term that might be misunderstood or even frowned on in academia. While play may not be readily seen in course catalogs, it certainly can be found in early childhood textbooks. The great majority of texts used in early childhood education courses include a chapter on play, and virtually all of them discuss it extensively in their coverage of learning environments, selection of materials, and curriculum.

According to Bowman there is more emphasis on play and more courses include it in programs for preparing teachers of preschool children, while play is not likely to be included in baccalaureate programs, especially those that focus exclusively on elementary education, excluding preschool education. My own experience corroborates this view; I have found that students who take specialized course work in early childhood education, even in four-year institutions, are exposed to some information about children's play. But those who take all of their course work in elementary education (the great majority of students, many of whom will teach kindergarten or primary children) rarely hear "play" discussed in their courses or see it mentioned in their textbooks.

Play is important to all young children—in kindergarten and primary as well as preschool classrooms. Teachers of young children can and should support and enhance children's play. But to do so they need to have an in-depth understanding of play and of the relationship between play and learning, an understanding best initiated in their education as teachers and enhanced during their years of work in classrooms through in-service education on "play and learning."

PREPARING TEACHERS
TO FACILITATE PLAY

The critical elements that must be included in early childhood teacher education programs that are to prepare teachers who have the awareness, knowledge, and skills to provide a rich and varied menu of appropriate play experiences for young children are described in this section. Teachers who understand the significance of play will develop strong positive attitudes toward it and commitment to providing opportunities for play in their classrooms. It is important that teacher educators model that they value play as the most important "work" of children and never let it be seen as a "frill" to be added to the curriculum after the "real work" is done.

To understand and appreciate the role of play in children's development, students need to learn about the history of early childhood education and the important role of play in the evolution of the field. It is also critically important that the study of child development be the cornerstone of early childhood teacher education programs. This study should include current information about play as a positive force in all aspects of children's development. New research on the role of play, especially the positive impact of sociodramatic play on school achievement, should be covered. College students also need to know about the different categories of play (for example, Smilansky's categories of functional play, constructive play, dramatic play, and games with rules) and some of the different schemes for classifying stages of play (for example, Parten and/or Smilansky).

Future teachers of young children also need to develop a wide repertoire of skills in facilitating play. "Children will play regardless of the circumstances. However, what you provide and how you interact with them during their play can make a vital difference in the quality and amount of play and what they learn in the process." (Feeney, Christensen, and Moravcik 1991, 104). Future teachers need to learn how to set the stage for play, observe and evaluate children's play, thoughtfully intervene to support the play, and include play in the planned curriculum.

Setting the Stage for Play

One of the most significant roles of the teacher in facilitating play is designing an environment that invites children to explore, to experiment with roles and materials, and to try new challenges. Teachers can learn to plan classrooms so that children have age-appropriate opportunities for all the different categories of play experiences. An environment that invites children to play includes adequate space indoors and outdoors, preferably organized into learning centers; sufficient and appropriate equipment and materials; and enough time to explore these in depth. Teachers need to appreciate and facilitate dramatic play and the use of blocks, for these are essential learning activities for young children. Teachers need to learn to let children control and direct their play themes and activities while setting reasonable limits to ensure that people and property are protected and that children feel safe from harm in the play environment.

Another aspect of setting the stage involves providing children experiences that give them raw material for their play. These experiences might include trips to places like the zoo, hospital, or construction site; visitors to the classroom; discussions of things of interest to children; and high-quality children's books that are read, discussed frequently, and available daily for children's independent use.

Observing and Evaluating Play

The second important role of the teacher is to observe and evaluate children's play. Observing play episodes tells the teacher a tremendous amount about individual children and about the group—interests, ways of learning, patterns of interaction, abilities, stage of development, ways of perceiving the world, and worries and fears. This knowledge is valuable in developing relationships with the children, in addressing issues of importance to them, and in designing meaningful and appropriate curriculum.

Careful and frequent observation also helps teachers know what can be done to support and extend play. Teachers observing play can tell if children need more time or more or different props for dramatic play or materials for constructive play, and what kinds of interventions they can make to enrich the play and to help children engage more fully in the play process.

College students need extensive experience in observing children at play if they are to learn to appreciate its value and to facilitate it in their classrooms. They need ample time to observe children (informally and using structured observations) and to watch how skilled teachers prepare for and support play. Systematic observation can yield important insights about a child's stage of play development and about the level of play that is taking place in the classroom. Several checklists or scales have been developed for looking at play behavior. (Johnson, Christie, and Yawkey [1987] provide a good overview of available observation instruments.) It is beneficial for students if their teacher education programs include information about these techniques and opportunities for them to practice using them throughout their undergraduate preparation, not isolated to "one course on play" or one module in a specific course.

Intervening to Support Play

Until the 1960s the conventional wisdom was that teachers should not become directly involved in the play episodes of children. During the preceding decades, play was seen as the arena in which children were to be left free to work out their inner conflicts and exercise power over their environment that was denied them in their interactions with the adult world. Teachers were to keep out of the child's play world so as not to interfere with important psychological development. The only valid role allocated to the teacher was that of creator of the environment and careful observer of children's actions within the prepared environment.

Research in recent decades has pointed toward reasons for joining in children's play and ways to do so to extend play that is flagging or to support a child who needs to learn a new play skill (Feeney, Christensen, and Moravcik 1991). Research findings indicate that when teachers play with or alongside children they lend support to the amount and quality of the play (Smilansky 1968). Adult participation gives children a strong message that play is a valuable activity in its own right, so they play longer and learn new play behaviors from observing the adult. It also builds better rapport with the children when teachers learn more about them and become better able to interact with them around mutual interests. When teachers participate, the play episodes last much longer and become more elaborate (Johnson, Christie, and Yawkey 1987).

It is essential that children maintain control of the play and that teachers limit their role to actions and comments that extend and enrich the play. When teachers join in, they need to do so in a way that supports ongoing play. By asking questions, requesting service, and responding to things children have done, the teacher introduces new elements into the play without taking over.

Tutoring children in play skills has proven effective in improving the dramatic and sociodramatic play skills of children from low-income families. Improved play skills have been shown to be effective in bringing about gains in cognitive and social development (Smilansky 1990). Teacher preparation programs need to include ample opportunities for future teachers to learn skills in sensitively participating in children's play in ways that support and enrich it.

Including Play
in the Planned Curriculum

Through their exploration and self-initiated play activities, children construct knowledge, develop individual skills and interests, and form prosocial relationships in goal-directed activities. Young children need many opportunities to discover and learn through their play each day. Yet play in a planned environment cannot offer all the intellectual challenge needed by older preschoolers and kindergarten and primary age children. In addition to providing opportunities for child-chosen play, teachers of young children need to develop skill in planning learning experiences based on themes. The theme (or unit of study) is used as the *hub* around which appropriate activities are planned. Thematic planning allows teachers to integrate several different subject areas into meaningful and worthwhile experiences for children. Themes can involve children in active exploration and problem solving and help them deepen their understanding of the world. Children's lives and their environment—their families, cultures, community, or geographical locale—are good sources of themes. As children draw, paint, dictate and write stories, map with blocks, and act out roles, they are expressing their understanding of the working of a restaurant, farm, or hospital and are simultaneously developing skills in the context of play that is interesting and meaningful to them. Such thematically based play is particularly important in the primary classroom.

POLICIES NEEDED
TO SUPPORT PLAY

Important policy issues must be addressed if we are to preserve and expand play's place in children's lives. Strong professional commitments need to be forged in many arenas.

There is much that can and should be done to improve the ways that we teach about play in early childhood programs. "Administrators and practitioners need to acknowledge that teachers face Herculean battles as they attempt to implement play. Consequently, teachers need intense support and high-quality training to ensure that they understand . . ." (Kagan 1990, 183). Teacher training needs to focus on the preparation of teachers who have both the conviction and the skills to preserve the role of play in early childhood classrooms. Training needs to reflect the newest research and give students ample opportunity to observe children and to interact with them in play situations with regular feedback from a skilled supervisor. While the training of early childhood teachers to facilitate play is sometimes imperfect, it must be present in early childhood teacher training programs, and many teacher educators are committed to its improvement.

Many teachers trained in elementary education who have no specialized knowledge of child development and early childhood education are regularly hired in kindergarten and primary grade classrooms. If they are to provide the best possible educational experiences for young children, we need to make sure that all teachers who work with children from birth to eight years of age have received training above and beyond generic elementary education preparation and that this training is rich in the lore, value, and skills of children's play.

Certification patterns in many states make it possible for teachers with no training in early childhood education to be hired to teach kindergarten and primary grades. At present most states have some kind of early childhood certification, but it varies greatly in the age group covered and the kinds of training required, and it rarely guarantees that all teachers of young children will be appropriately trained. Dimidjian in *Early Childhood At Risk* recommends "the establishment of separate standards of licensing of early childhood programs and personnel, thereby ensuring developmental focus on curriculum and evaluation of programs. Separate certification, standards for early childhood educators are a necessity" (1989, 57). She further recommends the institution of separate and specific programs of teacher preparation for adults to work with children, birth through eight years.

If play is to be recognized as a worthwhile learning medium for young children, administrators and policymakers also need to be trained to recognize play's value and to support it in daily classroom practices, since they make hiring and curriculum decisions that have profound effects on the quality of children's educational experiences. Parents also need to be educated about the value of play so that they will learn to expect and demand it in their children's classrooms.

At the national level, a number of professional groups have given recent attention to early childhood education. Organizations including the National Association for the Education of Young Children (NAEYC), the National Association of State Boards of Education (NASBE), the Association for Supervision and Curriculum Development (ASCD), and the National Association of Elementary School Principals (NAESP), as well as the National Education Association (NEA), have recognized the importance of developmentally appropriate practice and specialized training for teachers of young children. Their efforts need to be continued, coalitions formed, and public information campaigns launched to gain support for the unique needs of young children and their right to learn through play. The pendulum is swinging in the direction of appropriate early childhood education. But much still needs to be done before the young children of our nation are taught in ways that research and theory have amply demonstrated are best for them.

REFERENCES

Bowman, B. 1990. Play in Teacher Education: The United States Perspective. In *Children's Play and Learning: Perspectives and Policy Implications,* edited by E. Klugman and S. Smilansky. New York: Teachers College Press.

Dimidjian, V. J. 1989. *Early Childhood At Risk: Actions and Advocacy for Young Children.* Washington, D.C.: National Education Association.

Feeney, S.; Christensen, D.; and Moravcik, E. 1991. *Who Am I in the Lives of Children?* 4th ed. Columbus, Ohio: Merrill.

Johnson, J. E.; Christie, J. F.; and Yawkey, T. D. 1987. *Play and Early Childhood Development.* Glenview, Ill.: Scott, Foresman.

Kagan, S. L. 1990. Children's Play: The Journey from Theory to Practice. In *Children's Play and Learning: Perspectives and Policy*

Implications edited by E. Klugman and S. Smilansky. New York: Teachers College Press.

Monighan-Nourot, P. 1990. The Legacy of Play in American Early Childhood Education. In *Children's Play and Learning: Perspectives and Policy Implications,* edited by E. Klugman and S. Smilansky. New York: Teachers College Press.

Monighan-Nourot, P.; Scales, B.; Van Hoorn, J.; and Almy, M. 1987. *Looking at Children's Play: The Bridge from Theory to Practice.* New York: Teachers College Press.

Parten, M. 1932. Social Participation Among Preschool Children. *Journal of Abnormal Psychology* 27, no. 3: 243–69.

Smilansky, S. 1968. *The Effects of Sociodramatic Play on Disadvantaged Preschool Children.* New York: Wiley.

————. 1990. Sociodramatic Play: Its Relevance to Behavior and Achievement in School. In *Children's Play and Learning: Perspectives and Policy Implications,* edited by E. Klugman and S. Smilansky. New York: Teachers College Press.

Smilansky, S., and Shefatya, L. 1990. *Facilitating Play: A Medium for Promoting Cognitive, Socio-Emotional and Academic Development in Young Children.* Gaithersburg, Md.: Psychosocial and Educational Publications.

CONCLUSION: SECURING PLAY'S PLACE IN PUBLIC EDUCATION TODAY

by Victoria Jean Dimidjian

The growth of early childhood classrooms—under the many titles used across the country ("Prekindergarten" or "Preprimary" or "3/4 nursery," for example)—and of separate divisions of early childhood within public education systems over the past decade is astounding. Those of us who lived parts of our professional lives in the quiet basements or the side wings of large buildings housing half-day nurseries or small parent cooperative preschools or community child care centers have been amazed at the growth in public education, reaching more children at ever-younger ages. Today more children start public school earlier than ever before; more children spend longer days being schooled than ever before; and more young children depend on adults outside the family for initial guidance in how to communicate, how to relate to others, how to think and act effectively, and how to earn a positive place in a daily life shared with others.

Are the classrooms and the child care centers in public schools ready to meet the challenges of educating very young children? Will the public system allow the best of the early childhood education tradition to enter the doorways where so many little feet are traveling? Will play have a valued place in the classrooms where three- to eight-year-olds begin to learn?

The answers to these questions lie with the teachers, administrators, and families in our communities across the country. And the answers will only be known over the next decade, will only be articulated affirmatively or negatively as we work during the decade of the 90s in the field of early education.

Teachers who agree with the research and practice presented in this volume must be part of the movement to assure that play is a valued component in the educational experience of every young child. Perhaps it will be reassuring to such teachers to know that in joining this effort, they are carrying on a tradition that has existed inside and outside the public education system since the beginning of the twentieth century. Carl Glickman (1984) has summarized the historical place of play in public education: "by looking at the span of preindustrial to contemporary times and by focusing on historical and social issues, we might better understand why play in school settings has always been a philosophical decision" (p. 256). In times when the dominant educational philosophy has been what Glickman terms either *experimental* or *existential,* two traditions that share much with early childhood in terms of conceptualization of knowledge and of the teaching-learning process, play has had a valued and central place in public school curricula for young children. Historically, the era of progressive education in the United States earlier in the twentieth century and the innovations of the 60s were expressions of such philosophical traditions. When the dominant philosophy has been *essentialism,* an approach that looks at acquisition of knowledge as a fixed, unidirectional, and simple transmittal process, however, play has been viewed as frivolous at best, nonproductive and noneducational at worst. Glickman notes that the early education curriculum in the post-sputnik era was "essentially playless," and much of what I have viewed during the 80s, such as "down-sizing the curriculum" and codified teaching, testing, and tracking procedures for children four to eight, rejects the possibility of play-filled classrooms.

Glickman identifies three possible courses of action for those who believe that play belongs in public education. The first is that educational advocates for play's place "can attempt to alter or enlarge the purpose of public schools so that experimental or existential learning is valued" (1984, 268). I support this, and I would urge teachers to go further: to articulate to parents and the community the valuable place of play so that support for play's place is affirmed within both the educational and the community systems in which children, teachers, and families live. Only in this way can the focus move from the anxious, rigid, too often autocratic back-to-basics trend that became dominant in the 80s toward a more affirming, developmental, teacher-authoritative basics-and-beyond approach that is characteristic of the best early education within and outside the public system.

But caution is in order. Such an approach must validate that young children are learning, that their basic skills are developing, and that their thinking, communicating, and creating competencies are strengthened. Testing data can support this and should not be neglected. But even more important are teacher observations, children's work samples, and portfolio presentations that show the accomplishments of children engaged in daily play activities. Such data must be compiled and used to show that play is a valuable vehicle for learning, not—as critics have charged—an excuse for teachers not to teach, a reason children don't learn.

In summary, then, teachers who believe in play's place must mobilize to assure that six key elements exist, that

- Their school systems articulate a thoughtful philosophical *commitment* to play in early childhood education;
- Their classrooms have *prepared environments* that provide the equipment, materials, space, and arrangement for productive play;
- Their *daily schedules* provide defined and sufficient blocks of time for children to initiate and complete play activities in all areas of the curriculum;
- Their own *competencies in observing and facilitating play* are sufficient to support most children's play initiatives and to intervene or to serve as play partners for those few children who can't begin or sustain play;
- Their *curriculum planning skills* are flexible enough to coordinate the explicit teaching experiences of the planned curriculum with the self-initiated play ideas that emerge from children's responses to the implicit play curriculum; and

- Their *advocacy skills* are capable of energetically expressing the importance of play's place in the curriculum and of communicating the children's achievements and skills in cognitive and social domains through play.

When all six of these elements are fully in place, early educators and the children in their classrooms will be assured of productive, play-filled learning opportunities from the moment that footsteps start down the hallways until voices fade from the environments where young children have worked so intensely in play.

REFERENCE

Glickman, C. 1984. Play in Public School Settings: A Philosophical Question. In *Child's Play: Developmental and Applied,* edited by T. Yawkey and A. Pellegrini. Hillsdale, N. J.: Erlbaum.

BIBLIOGRAPHY

Aries, P. 1962. *Centuries of Childhood: A Social History of Family Life.* New York: Knopf.

Curry, N. 1986. Where Have All the Players Gone? In *The Feeling Child: Affective Development Reconsidered,* edited by N. Curry. New York: Haworth Press.

Elkind, D. 1981. *The Hurried Child: Growing Up Too Fast Too Soon.* Reading, Mass.: Addison/Wesley.

———. 1987. *Miseducation: Preschoolers at Risk.* New York: Knopf.

Elkind, D., ed. 1991. *Perspectives on Early Childhood Education: Growing with Young Children Toward the 21st Century.* Washington, D.C.: National Education Association.

Fein, G. 1981. Pretend Play: An Integrative Review. *Child Development* 52: 1095–1118.

Garvey, C. 1977. *Play.* Cambridge: Harvard University Press.

Glickman, C. 1984. Play in Public School Settings: A Philosopical Question. In *Child's Play: Developmental and Applied,* edited by T. Yawkey and A. Pellegrini. Hillsdale, N.J.: Erlbaum.

Levinson, D. 1980. Toward a Conception of the Adult Life Course. In *Themes of Love and Work in Adulthood,* edited by N. Smelser and E. Erikson. Cambridge: Harvard University Press.

Neumann, E. 1971. *The Elements of Play.* New York: MSS Corp.

Postman, N. 1984. *The Disappearance of Childhood.* New York: Dell.

Singer, D., and Singer, J. 1990. *The House of Make-Believe: Children's Play and the Developing Imagination.* Cambridge: Harvard University Press.

Smelser, N., and Erikson, E., eds. 1980. *Themes of Love and Work in Adulthood.* Cambridge: Harvard University Press.

Sommerville, J. 1982. *The Rise and Fall of Childhood.* Beverly Hills/London/New Delhi: Sage Publications.

Suransky, V. 1982. *The Erosion of Childhood.* Chicago: University of Chicago Press.

Winn, M. 1983. *Children Without Childhood.* New York: Pantheon.

THE CONTRIBUTORS

William W. Anderson is Professor of Teacher Education at Shippensburg University in Pennsylvania. His major focus is literacy development and teaching of reading.

Sara Arnaud is Professor Emerita of Psychology in Child Development at the University of Pittsburgh. She has extensively investigated personality development in normal children.

Nancy Trevorrow Carbonara is a licensed psychologist who works at the Child Guidance Center and in private practice in Pittsburgh. Her special interest is in treatment of preschool children.

Nancy E. Curry is Professor of Child Development in the School of Social Work at the University of Pittsburgh. She is the coauthor of *Beyond Self-Esteem: Developing a Genuine Sense of Human Value.*

Victoria Jean Dimidjian is Professor of Early Childhood Education at Florida International University in Miami. She is the author of *Early Childhood At Risk: Actions and Advocacy for Young Children,* published by NEA.

Jana Dressden is a doctoral student in Early Childhood Education at the University of Georgia, where she is focusing on young children's cognition and play.

Stephanie Feeney is Professor of Education at the University of Hawaii at Manoa. She has served on the board of the National Association for the Education of Young Children, coauthored its "Code of Ethical Conduct," and written many teacher education materials, including *Who Am I in the Lives of Children?*

Greta G. Fein is Professor of Education in the Department of Curriculum and Instruction at the University of Maryland, where she has conducted research and writing on play and early education for many years.

Beatrice S. Fennimore is a member of the faculty at Indiana University of Pennsylvania. She is the author of *Child Advocacy for Early Childhood Educators,* and is at work on a book about young children in urban public schools.

Ann E. Fordham is Assistant Professor of Teacher Education at Shippensburg University in Pennsylvania, where she teaches early childhood and language arts/reading courses.

Constance Kamii is Professor of Early Childhood Education at the University of Alabama at Birmingham. She is a coeditor of *Early Literacy: A Constructivist Foundation for Whole Language,* published by NEA.

Barbara A. Lewis is an Assistant Professor in the Department of Curriculum and Instruction at the University of Alabama at Birmingham.

Alicia Mendoza is Chair of Elementary Education at Florida International University in Miami, where she teaches primarily in the area of early childhood education.

Anthony D. Pellegrini is Professor of Early Childhood Education at the University of Georgia. His research interest is in children's play in preschool and primary years.

Fred Rogers is creator and host of the PBS children's television series "Mister Rogers' Neighborhood." In addition to his background in music composition, television production, and Presbyterian ordination, he also studied child development intensively with Margaret McFarland, who was psychological consultant for "the neighborhood" until her death in 1988.

Joyce Rubin is an Adjunct Instructor at Florida International University, specializing in work with student interns and student teachers in the public schools of South Florida.

Mary Ellen Sapp is Program Professor of Education and Director of Practicums for Programs in Child and Youth Studies, Center for Advancement of Education, at Nova University in Fort Lauderdale, Florida.

Paula Scanlon teaches kindergarten in suburban Pittsburgh. She completed degrees in early childhood education and child development and has also taught in child care.

Thomas Schultz is Director of Early Childhood Education for the National Association of State Boards of Education, Alexandria, Virginia. He is the coauthor of the 1989 NASBE report *Right from the Start.*

Hedda Bluestone Sharapan is Associate Producer of "Mister Rogers' Neighborhood" and has been on its staff since 1966.

Edwina B. Vold is Professor of Early Childhood Education and Chair of the Department of Professional Studies at Indiana University of Pennsylvania. Her current research focuses on multicultural education. She is the editor of *Multicultural Education in Early Childhood Classrooms,* published by NEA.

Karen West teaches second grade at Estig Elementary School, part of the Tampa (Florida) Public Schools.

Charles H. Wolfgang is Associate Professor of Education at Florida State University in Tallahassee. He is the coauthor of *School for Young Children,* which examines play curriculum for three- to five-year-olds.